T0093821

ETHICAL MACHINES

ETHICAL MACHINES

Your Concise Guide to Totally Unbiased, Transparent, and Respectful AI

REID BLACKMAN

Harvard Business Review Press
Boston, Massachusetts

HBR Press Quantity Sales Discounts

Harvard Business Review Press titles are available at significant quantity discounts when purchased in bulk for client gifts, sales promotions, and premiums. Special editions, including books with corporate logos, customized covers, and letters from the company or CEO printed in the front matter, as well as excerpts of existing books, can also be created in large quantities for special needs.

For details and discount information for both print and ebook formats, contact booksales@harvardbusiness.org, tel. 800-988-0886, or www.hbr.org/bulksales.

Copyright 2022 Reid Blackman
All rights reserved
Printed in the United States of America

10 9 8 7 6 5 4 3 2 1

No part of this publication may be reproduced, stored in or introduced into a retrieval system, or transmitted, in any form, or by any means (electronic, mechanical, photocopying, recording, or otherwise), without the prior permission of the publisher. Requests for permission should be directed to permissions@harvardbusiness.org, or mailed to Permissions, Harvard Business School Publishing, 60 Harvard Way, Boston, Massachusetts 02163.

The web addresses referenced in this book were live and correct at the time of the book's publication but may be subject to change.

Library of Congress Cataloging-in-Publication Data
Names: Blackman, Reid, author.
Title: Ethical machines : your concise guide to totally unbiased, transparent, and respectful AI / Reid Blackman.
Description: Boston, Massachusetts : Harvard Business Review Press, [2022] | Includes index. |
Identifiers: LCCN 2022003876 (print) | LCCN 2022003877 (ebook) | ISBN 9781647822811 (hardcover) | ISBN 9781647822828 (epub)
Subjects: LCSH: Artificial intelligence—Moral and ethical aspects. | Computer algorithms—Moral and ethical aspects. | Data privacy. | Discrimination. | Computers and civilization.
Classification: LCC Q334.7 .B53 2022 (print) | LCC Q334.7 (ebook) | DDC 174/.90063—dc23/eng20220322
LC record available at https://lccn.loc.gov/2022003876
LC ebook record available at https://lccn.loc.gov/2022003877

ISBN: 978-1-64782-281-1
eISBN: 978-1-64782-282-8

The paper used in this publication meets the requirements of the American National Standard for Permanence of Paper for Publications and Documents in Libraries and Archives Z39.48-1992.

To Riva (aka "Little") and Remy (aka "Badagooch" aka "Bada" aka "Gorgeous Guy" aka "Gorge"), who are living proof that I can love things that make unfair demands, operate as black boxes, and so flagrantly violate my privacy that not even the bathroom is a safe haven.

TABLE OF CONTENTS

ETHICAL MACHINES

INTRODUCTION

AI for ~~Good~~ Not Bad

The word that echoes in my head is "squishy." Squishy. You can't get a grip on it. It's here for a second, but you try to hold it and—woops!—it's squirted out the sides. If only it were harder, more concrete, you could *do* something with it. But this squishy mass—it just invites confusion, sometimes frustration, and ultimately, resignation.

But it was the word a senior executive used to describe AI ethics when he explained why they weren't doing much about it. His first order of business? Invite speakers to come and talk about the squishiness. Maybe they could help him corner the goo until it had nowhere to go. And maybe other speakers could help with other alleged properties of ethics that this and other executives often associate with the topic: "fuzzy," "theoretical," "abstract," and "subjective."

The executive conceived of himself, as do scientists and engineers, as someone who deals with cold, hard facts. You can do things with those. You can discover them. You can infer things from them. You can track them. Ethics, on the other hand, is apparently a stew of hot, soft, nonfacts. The only thing to do is to mop it up and throw it in the trash, or perhaps wait around in hopes that it will dry and you can sweep it under the rug.

But the scientists and engineers, and this executive, are wrong. Ethics is not squishy and there is plenty you can do with it. You can articulate a set of goals with it. You can devise strategies to achieve those goals and deploy tactics that realize those strategies. If you're particularly averse to the ethical and reputational risks of AI or you want to be known for being at the cutting edge of ethical AI, you can drive it into every facet of your organization. The goal of this book is to teach you how to think about ethics, what you need to know about AI ethics in particular, and how to—well, not *drive* it; that seems a bit too violent for successful organizational change, so let's say—*nestle* it into operations. I won't only tell you what to do, though. I'll teach you how to think about the topic so that you'll see what you need to do. By the time we're done, I'll have revealed the landscape of AI ethics to you and you'll be equipped with the requisite tools for navigating a map you'll have already internalized.

How do I know I can get you there? Because I've been researching, publishing, and teaching on ethics in general, and AI ethics in particular, for more than twenty years. First, as a professor of philosophy, and second, as an adviser and consultant on AI ethics for senior leaders in organizations ranging from *Fortune* 500 companies to nonprofits to startups, in sectors as varied as health care, financial services, insurance, and more. In both of these roles, my job has not been to act as a kind of ethical oracle, in which I impart my own ethical views. Instead, my mission is to enable others to make informed and wise ethical decisions. And between working with all those companies and having my own businesses, I've learned quite a bit about how to make AI ethics actionable and compatible with real-world business necessities. In fact, you'll see examples of that throughout this book, as I take you into the ethical AI issues my clients face and how I've steered them to safety.

Why AI Ethics?

Let's not get ahead of ourselves, though. Why even talk about AI ethics? Or better: Why talk about it in a business setting? Why should board members, C-suites, product owners and managers, engineers, data scientists, and students of such things—the intended audience of this book—*care* about AI ethics? Yes, sure, ethics is important and let's all hold hands and sing hallelujah, but why is AI ethics getting so much attention and why does it deserve yours, in your capacity not only as a human being but also as an employer and employee?

It's helpful to distinguish "AI for Good" from "AI for Not Bad." Those who rally around the former want to use the new tool that we call artificial intelligence (more on this soon) to create a "positive social impact." This means doing things like creating AI that aids in educating people in developing countries or identifying alternative sources of energy or lifting people out of poverty. These are all noble goals, and the people who pursue them are to be applauded.

AI for Not Bad, on the other hand, concerns itself with avoiding ethical pitfalls in one's pursuit of one's goals, whether those goals are ethically admirable or ethically neutral. For example, if you're creating an AI to read the tens of thousands of résumés your organization receives, that is a fairly neutral goal when it comes to ethics; you'll receive no great moral praise for your efficient dispatching of your task. But if you do it in a way that leads to, say, systemically discriminating against women and people of color, that's a bad thing. The AI for Not Bad people want to ensure that bad stuff doesn't happen in the development, procurement, and ultimately, the deployment of AI, whatever your purposes happen to be. (Of course, you might have ethically bad goals, but then you probably don't care very much about the means to those ends, in which case you're not an AI for Not Bad person, either.)

Put slightly differently, AI for Not Bad is about risk mitigation. Ethical risk mitigation. And when it comes to AI, there are loads of ethical risks that need mitigating.

Plenty of companies have already learned this the hard way:

- An Uber self-driving car killed a woman.[1]
- Regulators are investigating Optum Healthcare for creating an AI that recommends doctors and nurses pay more attention to white patients than to sicker Black patients.[2]
- Goldman Sachs was under investigation for creating an AI that sets credit limits for its Apple card lower for women than for men. Ultimately, Goldman was exonerated, but not before a round of negative press.
- Amazon abandoned a résumé-reading AI after two years because it couldn't figure out how to stop it from discriminating against women.[3]
- Facial-recognition companies have faced bans by cities across the country and a raft of negative press.[4]

- Northpointe created AI software that systematically discriminates against Black people in determining risk ratings for crime that affected judges' sentencing and bail decisions.[5]
- Facebook . . . well, there's just a lot there.

The list goes on. And what one sees is that ethical risks are not only bad in themselves or, more specifically, bad for the people who are wronged by the ethically disastrous effects of AI gone bad, but also pose significant reputational, regulatory, and legal risks. What's particularly alarming is that the risks are always large in scope precisely because AI operates at scale. That's one of the reasons for developing AI in the first place: it does tasks in mere seconds that would take humans hundreds of hours. It can do a lot of calculating, fast. That means when an ethical risk is realized, it never affects just one person. Rather, it affects the massive set of people on whom you deploy it: everyone who applies to that job or applies for a mortgage or loan; anyone in the path of your self-driving car; anyone your facial-recognition camera spots; anyone who sees or does not see your job ad (in cases of discrimination); anyone at your hospital who is diagnosed by AI software; anyone your AI directs you to market to. And on and on. So, given the scope of potential applications for AI, which is enormous, the rate at which AI scales, which is blinding, and the array of things that can go ethically wrong in the development and deployment of AI, which is vast, one cannot help but ask the following questions:

- How much time and how many resources does it take to respond to a regulatory investigation?
- How many millions are spent paying a fine if you've been found guilty, let alone negligent, of violating regulations or laws?

- How many hundreds of millions of dollars does a brand need to spend to rebuild trust?

That's why this book is for such a wide swath of people. If you're on the board or in the C-suite, you're responsible for ensuring that wide-scale and deep ethical risks don't tarnish your organization's brand or invite regulatory investigation and lawsuits. If you're a product owner or manager of an AI team, or you're an engineer or a data scientist, you don't want to be responsible for invasions of privacy, inadvertently discriminating against women and people of color, or manipulating people into spending more money than they can afford. In fact, if you're an employee of an organization that develops or procures AI, you probably don't want to work for a company that takes these things lightly, even if you're not directly involved in developing or procuring AI.

Isn't There a Code of Conduct or Regulations to Deal with This?

You'd be forgiven for thinking that there are already proper pieces in place to take care of this. Corporate codes of conduct urge good judgment, integrity, and high ethical standards. There are antidiscrimination laws and, for instance, when it comes to self-driving cars, laws against killing and maiming pedestrians, even if it's a bit rainy. Does AI ethics really require a separate treatment?

Well, if it doesn't, this is a big waste of paper. As it happens, it does.

Corporate codes of conduct govern people's behavior so that they can be aware of what behaviors are on and off the menu. People know, for the most part, how not to do bad things. If they don't, there is training that can be offered. In the case of AI, though, ethical risks are not realized as a result of bad behavior. It's the result of not thinking through the consequences, not monitoring the AI "in the wild," not knowing what one should be on the lookout for when developing or procuring AI. Put slightly differently, while the ethical risks of AI are not novel—discrimination, invasions of privacy, manslaughter, and so on have been around since time immemorial—AI creates novel paths to realize those risks. This means we need novel ways to block those paths from being traveled.

A similar line of thought applies in the case of law and regulations. Since there are new ways to break the law, new techniques need to be created to stop well-intentioned but would-be lawbreakers. That's easier said than done. As we'll see in a later chapter, some of the techniques for mitigating AI ethical risks actually run afoul of current law or operate in a way that is legally unproblematic but ethically, and so reputationally, dangerous. That means organizations can be in the unenviable position of having to decide either to deploy an ethically risky but legally compliant AI, an ethically sound but illegal AI, or to withhold from deploying it at all.

A Crash Course in AI

Let's get clear on some terms. When people talk about AI in pop culture, they're often talking about the kinds of robots you see in *Terminator*. They have consciousness, they have questionable motives, they're destructive, and so on. In the world of engineering and computer science, this is called "artificial general intelligence (AGI)," and some people—Elon Musk and Stephen Hawking, for example—think that AGI is going to lead to the destruction of humanity. That's because an AGI would be highly adaptive. It would set its own goals instead of having humans tell it what to pursue; maybe it would aim for annihilation. It might be capable of a level of multitasking that humans aren't capable of; maybe it would replace human utility in the workplace. It could outpunch Rocky, outsmart Sherlock, and out-oppress Pol Pot.

But AGI doesn't exist now, and it's hotly debated whether it ever will. Suffice it to say that most, myself included, think we are a long way from creating an AGI, if we ever will.

What we have now is called "artificial narrow intelligence." The task that any given ANI can handle is relatively . . . wait for it . . . narrow. For example, it can determine health insurance premiums but nothing else, unless combined with another ANI. It's inflexible. It pursues a goal that the human developers give it. It has no desires for world domination, for peace, or anything in between. In a way, it's sort of stupid. The calculator on your phone can do mathematical calculations in fractions of a second that you couldn't do in your lifetime but doesn't know that two cookies are better than one, as my two-year-old does. My two-year-old is also extraordinarily unlikely to confuse a soccer ball with someone's bald head; not so with a "ball-tracking" AI.[6]

So ANI is what we have. More specifically, the vast majority of ANI around now that businesses have developed and deployed at an alarming rate worldwide is called "machine learning," or ML. We'll get into some details of how ML works in later chapters. For now, we need to understand the basics to see how those novel paths to ethical risks get created.

The first thing to note is that we're really just talking about software, which you're likely quite familiar with. Microsoft Word,

Gmail, GarageBand, Call of Duty, and Pornhub: all examples of software. You can use them to create content, view content, and if you're into it, both.

Underlying that software is computer code. Now there are all sorts of computer code and techniques computer engineers use to create that code. One such technique is using an algorithm, or "algo." Algorithms, in concept, are simple. They're mathematical equations that take some input, do some calculations with that input, and then give an output. Maybe you have an algorithm that just adds two to any number you input into it. So, you take the number four, pop it into your algo, and it spits out six. It's very impressive.

Some algorithms are quite complicated. Insurance companies have complicated algos to determine your premium, for example. They take some inputs—age, sex, driving record, and so on—pop it into their proprietary algorithm, and the algorithm outputs a premium.

Back in the 1950s, some computer scientists learned to make a very interesting kind of algorithm: a "machine learning" algorithm. Machine learning algorithms work differently from standard algorithms. With the latter, you determine exactly how the inputs will be treated such that a particular output will be generated. The person who made an insurance premium algorithm determines what the inputs are and how much each one should matter or weigh. For instance, perhaps you choose that age should count twice as much as sex or driving record should count as three times more important than zip code, and so on. But with machine learning, you do no such thing. Instead—and in a way this is what's so shockingly simple about machine learning—machine learning is just learning by example.

Suppose you want your ML-powered software to tell you

whether the picture you just uploaded is a picture of a dog. First thing you need to do is *train* your ML. You begin by taking a thousand pictures of dogs, inputting them into your ML algorithm, and then you tell it, "These are all pictures of dogs. Find what they have in common—find the 'dog pattern' that's present in all of them." Your ML then crawls through all those photos and finds a pattern they all have. Then you give it photo #1001, which is a picture of your new dog, and tell the AI, "If this has the dog pattern (if it's a picture that's sufficiently similar to those first photos I gave you), tell me it's a dog. If not, tell me it's not a dog." If the ML does a good job, it'll tell you photo #1001 is a dog. If it does a not-so-great job (and more later on how it might fail to do a great job), it will say it's not a dog.

If it turns out it says, "not dog," then you can correct it. "Actually, ML, that's a dog, too." Then your ML will go look for a new pattern, one that is had by photos #1–#1001. And you just keep going. It learns by example, and the more examples you give it, all else equal, the better it gets. Why do you think Google keeps asking you to click on the pictures with a car in it to verify that you're a person? You're *labeling* those photos so it can get more examples to feed its ML so its ML gets better at recognizing when there's a car in a picture. You should have invoiced Google years ago.

To be clear, this is totally amazing. Compare it to what we'd have to do without these programs that learn by example. We'd have to write some insanely long sentence (in a computer programming language), like, "If it has two eyes and two ears and the eyes are *x* inches apart and blah blah blah, then label it 'dog.'" But trying to get this right would take forever. We'd never do it. There are other animals with two eyes and two ears (cats, wolves . . . human beings), some dogs are missing an ear or an eye, and so on. Much easier to say, "Look, label 'dog' anything that looks like these things," and let the AI figure it out. Turns out, it's a lot more accurate, too.

You might be wondering why AI is all the rage now if ML algorithms were developed in the 1950s. The main reasons have to do with processing power and the availability of data. As you can see, ML works well when it has lots of data to learn from, where that data is digitized. With the advent of the digital revolution, including the extent to which the internet has woven itself into almost every facet of life, comes a tremendous amount of data already digitized and thus usable for training ML algorithms. That said, even if, *per impossible*, computer scientists had all that data back then, they couldn't do anything with it. That's because computers didn't have the processing power to crunch those vast troves of data. So, in short: old algorithms + a bonkers quantity of digitized data + insane computing power = today's AI (and ML) revolution.

The Big Three

Walk into any conference where AI ethics is discussed and you can't help but hear repeated references to three topics above all others: biased AI, black-box algorithms, and creepy violations of privacy. These are, by far, the most talked about problems in AI ethics because these issues are highly correlated with AI software applications. The explanation for the correlation consists in how the unique technique that is ML gives rise to those ethical risks. Let's take these in turn.

Privacy

Suppose you're developing an AI and you want it to be incredibly accurate. You're going to want to get as much data as you can to train your AI. That's going to be data about me, your friends, your family, and just about anyone else. In other words, the fuel of ML is data, and it's often data about people. So, you—or rather, the companies that developers work for—are highly incentivized to suck up as much data about as many people as possible. That data is useful not only for doing standard data analytics—analyzing data to gain insight into, say, your average customer profile—but also for training your AI. Again, it's not as though privacy violations didn't exist before AI, but rather that any push for creating AI solutions cannot help but also be a push to get more data about more people, thereby encouraging invasions of privacy. What's more, by virtue of gathering data from multiple sources, an AI can make true inferences about people that those people do not want companies to know about them.

Explainability

ML takes massive troves of data, "recognizes" a pattern or patterns in that data, and compares that pattern against novel inputs in order to make a "prediction" about it, for example, the likelihood of missing payments on a mortgage, of committing a crime in the next two years, of being a person who might click on this ad, and so on. The trouble is that the patterns are often so complex or cover a range of variables so different from what we usually pay attention to, that we often cannot explain why the AI gave the output that it did. That dog-recognizing software, for instance, analyzes each of those dog pictures at the pixel level. We humans, of course, don't look at pictures at the pixel level, and even if we did, there are far too many pixels for us to keep track of in order to determine what patterns emerge among them. Similarly, using AI, a company might not know why it declined that request for a mortgage, why it issued that credit limit, or why it gave this person and not that person a job ad or an interview. You may have heard the phrase "black-box algorithms"—this is the problem it's referring to.

Bias

If you've heard anything about AI ethics, then you've heard about biased or discriminatory algorithms. The general problem is that an AI can give outputs that have ethically (and, in some cases, legally) unacceptable differential impacts across various subpopulations, and this can happen without any intention of the engineers to discriminate. Indeed, it can happen even in the presence of intentions to avoid discrimination. There is much to be said here, covered in detail in chapter 2, but an example is worth exploring to bring out the problem.

Suppose you receive tens of thousands of résumés every day. Rather than have humans engage in the laborious process of vetting all of them, you want to train an AI to read them and green-light the résumés that should lead to an interview and red-light those that should not. In that case, the first thing you'll need is data to train your AI, and luckily, you happen to have quite a bit: the last ten years or so of hiring data within your organization, including digitized copies of all the résumés that were green-lit and red-lit. So you give your AI all those résumés, being sure to include in your inputs which résumés led to an interview and which did not after humans reviewed them—this is called "labeled data"—and tell your AI to look for the "interview worthy" pattern.

When Amazon did this, its AI learned a pattern it wished it hadn't, which was, roughly, *we don't hire women here.* As a result, the AI red-lit new résumés by women, for instance, by noticing things like "Women's NCAA Basketball."

We can ask a variety of questions about why the previous years of hiring data reflected that Amazon tends not to hire women. That could be the result of discriminatory hiring managers. It could be the result of a general women-in-tech pipeline problem that Amazon inherited, which may or may not reflect a misogynistic culture in tech or in STEM disciplines generally. It could be because men are more likely to lie on their résumés than women. It could be all of these things or some of these things and more. We don't need to decide that here. All we have to know is that the pattern was there, the AI recognized it independently of any intentions of the engineers training the AI, and the AI offered discriminatory recommendations as a result. (This example also brings out why a code of conduct requiring good behavior is a nonstarter.)

The Amazon engineers attempted to fix the AI so it did not discriminate against women, and later we'll dive into some of the details. But just know for now that they couldn't do it, and to Amazon's and the engineers' great credit, they abandoned the project to which they had dedicated hundreds of thousands of dollars in labor (not to mention the processing costs of training and retraining an algorithm, which are quite significant).

That's another reason to take the ethical risks of AI seriously: if you don't know how to handle them, you can waste a lot of time and money developing software that is ultimately too risky to use or sell.

Comprehensiveness and the Structure-Content Distinction

Privacy, explainability, and bias are the big three challenges of AI ethics. But not all of the ethical risks of AI fall neatly into those three categories. Those categories are standardly highlighted in discussions of AI ethics because they are particularly relevant by virtue of how ML works. The truth is that some of the biggest ethical risks of AI are the result of the particular uses to which the technology is put.

Surveillance (by facial-recognition technology, to name one example) is a problem because it destroys trust, causes anxiety, alters people's behavior, and ultimately erodes autonomy. Questions about whether people are being treated respectfully, whether some product design is manipulative or merely giving reasonable incentives, whether some decision would be cruel or (culturally) insensitive, whether a decision places a burden on people that is too great to reasonably expect of them . . . these are all ethical issues that can arise depending on the use case of an AI. And there are many, many more.

In my estimation, the nearly all-consuming interest in the big three challenges by the AI ethics community (save for concerns about particular use cases, like facial-recognition software) has created a danger in itself. It encourages a lopsided approach to identifying ethical risks, which naturally invites failures at identifying those risks. This in turn has led companies to think they're already "doing AI ethics" because they vet for bias and try to build explainable models. But aside from the fact that they usually get these things wrong—more on this later—they simply are not looking at the whole risky picture. We need a *comprehensive* approach.

A crucial distinction for understanding AI ethics, particularly in the context of putting AI ethics into practice, is Structure versus Content.

An organization that vets for AI ethical risks needs a governance *Structure*. There will be policies, processes, role-specific responsibilities, and more. Put differently, an organization that has an AI ethical risk program or implemented framework has a set of mechanisms in place to identify and mitigate the ethical risks it may realize in the development, procurement, and deployment of AI. It consists in the set of things one will reference in answer to the question, "*How* does your organization identify and mitigate the ethical risks of AI?"

On the other hand, the ethical risks that the company wants to avoid constitute the *Content* of its program. Most in the AI ethics community are committed to a program that includes in that Content respecting people's privacy, making the outputs of all ML explainable, and ensuring that the ML delivers fair or equitable (i.e., unbiased) outputs.

The distinction between Structure and Content can be made clear by considering an extreme example. Imagine an organization with an absolutely enviable AI Ethics Structure. The role-specific responsibilities of data collectors, engineers, data scientists, product managers, and so on are crystal clear. The means by which they elevate concerns to senior leadership are tried and true. There's an ethics committee that carries out its tasks in complete earnestness. It's a mechanistic marvel.

Now take that Structure and pop it into an organization like the Ku Klux Klan. It turns out, it's marvelous at ensuring its data sets are biased in a way that favors white people and especially white men, it ensures the obscurity of decisions about prison sentences for Black people, and it makes products that are particularly good at surveilling members of the LGBTQ community.

The example brings the distinction between Structure and Content into stark relief. Structure concerns the way you identify and mitigate ethical risks. Content concerns what you take those ethical risks to be. An effective AI ethical risk program includes both.

We got to this distinction because we were talking about the big three challenges of AI ethics, and I noted that there are many more ethical risks than those three. Overly emphasizing them, I said, results in a lopsided approach to identifying and mitigating ethical risks. We need comprehensiveness. More specifically, we need AI ethical risk programs that reflect a deep understanding of all the ethical risks we are trying to avoid (Content) and leave no stone unturned in looking for them (Structure). We cannot let our concern for the big three eclipse either what we're looking for or how we look for it.

This stands in contrast to how most companies approach AI ethics, if they approach it at all. That approach consists in getting concerned about bias in particular and then using a technical tool to identify bias so various bias-mitigation techniques can be used. I'll discuss this in detail in a later chapter, but we can already see how narrow this approach is.

What's to Come

Almost every discussion of AI ethics begins with decrying the existence of biased, unexplainable, privacy-violating AI while expressing outrage at the companies that produce them. Those people are addressing the Content issue. The conversation then immediately pivots to techniques or tools that developers can use to mitigate ethical risks. The implicit assumption in that pivot is that we understand the Content issues well enough to get to work mitigating the risks. This assumption is false.

Even those who spend a lot of time talking about and even working in the field of AI ethics have a lot of difficulty understanding what's to be done. That is because they're trying to build Structure around something they still find squishy, fuzzy, and subjective. They're doing AI ethical risk mitigation, and while they may know a lot about AI and a lot about risk mitigation, they don't know much about ethics.

The contention I defend throughout this book is that you will never get a robust and comprehensive Structure if you don't understand ethics, that is, if you don't understand the Content side of things. In fact, my thesis is even stronger than that: understanding the Content makes the Structure of an AI ethics program easy to see.

This is a point I will keep hammering home. Once you come to appreciate what the risks are and where they come from, it's no great leap to figure out what to do about it. Everyone is going around with their hair on fire screaming, "How do we operationalize AI ethics? What do we do?!" And my reaction is, "Calm down. You're only worked up because you don't understand enough about (AI) ethics. If you did, you'd see it's not that hard." You can (loosely speaking) derive knowledge about what to do once you're well informed about the issues and where they come from. Understand Content and the Structure stuff becomes fairly obvious.

The reason people can't see the Structure now is that it's covered in a fog of conceptual confusion, conflated questions, and good old (nonculpable) ignorance. It's hard to know what to build when you don't understand the foundations or where you're building. I'm going to help lift the fog to reveal the landscape of AI ethics, and I'm going to do it largely by helping you to understand the Content side of things. You'll see the terrain and be able to navigate it.

We'll start, in chapter 1, by turning squishy ethics into something concrete. I'll explain how a number of confusions have led people to think of ethics as subjective, which is problematic not only because the truth matters, but because thinking about ethics as hard and objective is extremely useful in the context of building an AI ethical risk program.

Chapters 2 through 4 tackle the big three challenges of AI ethics, one per chapter. As we'll see, these issues are a lot more than scary stories in the news and social media, and going deep on understanding how those issues arise and why they're important will go a long way in instructing us how to mitigate them.

In chapter 5 I'll tell you how to create an AI ethics statement that actually guides actions (instead of functioning, at best, as PR) by articulating values in light of the kinds of actions your organization sees as ethically out of bounds.

Chapter 6 is an explicit articulation of the Structure of an effective, comprehensive, scalable AI ethical risk program. You can see that chapter as a kind of *conclusion* that can be drawn from chapters 1 through 5, which are Content chapters.

Finally, chapter 7 focuses on a particular area in your Structure: your product team, and how they should think about Content if they're going to get their job done well.

I'm not going to lie: there's a lot here to digest. To make it a bit easier, I've given you a list of key takeaways. If you understand the rationale behind each one of them, you'll see the AI ethics landscape with ease.

It's time for the first step in lifting that fog: undoing the dogma about the subjectivity of ethics. Let's get to it.

Recap

- AI ethics can be split into two domains: AI for Good and AI for Not Bad. The former is an attempt to create positive social impact. The latter is about ethical risk mitigation.
- Ethical risks are not only bad because doing the wrong thing is bad. The ethical risks that companies can realize in their use of AI are also reputational, regulatory, and legal risks that could cost a company hundreds of millions in fines and legal fees, not to mention a tremendous amount of time and something it is notoriously difficult to regain once lost: client and consumer trust.
- AI ethical risk mitigation is not well suited to be taken care of by a code of conduct. Bad behavior by employees is not the issue.
- Current regulations and laws do not cover all of the ethical risks that can damage a brand, and they almost certainly never will.
- AI ethical risks in business are, for now and the foreseeable future, the result of developing artificial narrow intelligence (ANI) and, more specifically, machine learning (ML).
- The big three challenges of AI ethics are privacy violations, explainability, and bias. They are not, however, the only ethical

risks of AI. Many ethical risks arise from the countless use cases for AI (e.g., facial recognition and self-driving cars).

- We should distinguish between the Structure and the Content of an AI ethics program. The Structure speaks to the formal mechanisms in place for identifying and mitigating ethical risks. The Content speaks to what the organization takes to be ethically risky or, put slightly differently, what the organization takes to be ethically good and bad. Having a firm grip on the Content makes it easy to see what a good Structure looks like.

1

Here's How You Should Think about Ethics

This book gives you advice on how to build, procure, and deploy AI in an ethically (and thus reputationally, regulatory, and legally) safe way, and to do it at scale. We're not here to tackle existential and metaphysical questions like, "How does AI affect what we should think about what it is to be human?" or "What does AI teach us about the nature of consciousness?" That said, we cannot get clear direction without clear conceptual foundations. This chapter lays those foundations.

The senior executive who described AI ethics as "squishy" wasn't some rube. He was a person with a long and successful career in risk and compliance. And the others who describe it as "fuzzy" and "subjective" likewise are smart, accomplished people.

As a former professor of philosophy, I heard these sentiments for nearly twenty years. I now see them again with my clients and whenever people talk about AI ethics in almost any context. And when I do hear it, I'm quick to point out that such a mindset stymies progress.

When people say ethics is squishy—or as I'll say from now on, "subjective"—they're effectively saying that they're not quite sure how to think about it, and they usually give up trying.

It's particularly difficult for senior leaders trying to effect change within their organization. Those leaders are trying to create a comprehensive AI ethical risk program, which requires buy-in at every level of the organization. They often have the experience of walking into a room of engineers, telling them AI ethics is really important, and then facing the inevitable question, "But isn't ethics subjective?"

This is the kiss of death. Engineers tend to like things that are concrete, quantifiable, empirically verifiable. Whatever is not that doesn't deserve their intellectual attention or care. That senior leader talking about AI ethics? That's just PR. That's political correctness getting in the way of technological progress. It's touchy-feely stuff that has no place in a conversation among serious people, and certainly not in business.

The leader who doesn't know how to respond to such protestations is in trouble. If they say, "Well, yes, it's subjective, but . . ." they've already lost. So senior leaders need to get this right if they are to get the organizational buy-in they'll need to drive—sorry, nestle—AI ethics throughout operations.

That's just the beginning, though. You'll also need people to think about ethics in a way that isn't met with a shrug whenever they need to do some ethical thinking, as required by the AI ethics program you'll put in place; in performing ethical-risk due diligence during product development, for instance, or in the deliberations by an ethics committee.

So, getting your people to think about AI ethics as something other than subjective is imperative both for organizational buy-in and for the sake of effective ethical risk analysis during product development, procurement, and deployment. As it happens, there is a very good reason for you and your team to stop thinking of ethics as subjective and to start thinking of it in a way that lends itself to fruitful discussions and, ultimately, risk identification and mitigation. Put slightly differently, if you're prone to talk about "responsible AI," then you'll need to think about ethics in a way that lends itself to responsible inquiry into the ethical risks of AI. And put differently one more time for those of you in the back seats: AI ethics is about two things—AI and ethics. In the previous chapter we got clarity on what AI or ML is and how it works. Now it's time to get clear on ethics.

Don't worry: I'm not going to write a philosophical treatise here. Turns out, all you need to think about ethics effectively is to get clarity on *a question*, *a confusion*, and *three notoriously bad but ubiquitous reasons for thinking ethics is subjective*. Once we do that, off we go to putting ethics into practice.

The Question

One question I get a lot is "What is ethics?" The inquirer is standardly looking for a "definition" of ethics. They might even ask, "How do you define 'ethics'?" or "What's your definition of 'ethics'?"

But my view of how to get a grip on what ethics is *about*—and this is really what the inquirer is after—is to think about some of the core questions that we naturally characterize as *ethical* questions, like these:

- What is a good life?
- Do we have any obligations to each other? What are they?
- Is compassion a virtue? Courage? Generosity?
- Is abortion ethically permissible? Capital punishment? Euthanasia?
- What is privacy and do people have a right to it?
- What is discrimination and what makes it bad?
- Do people have equal moral worth?
- Do individuals have an obligation to engage in self-improvement?
- Is it ever ethically permissible to lie?
- Do corporations have obligations to their employees? To society at large?
- Is Facebook unreasonably incentivizing or manipulating its users into clicking on ads?
- Is it ethically permissible to use black-box algorithms to diagnose illnesses?

And so on. What is ethics? Well, don't worry about a definition of the term—if you really want a definition, just look it up in a dictionary. If you want to know what ethics is about, think about these kinds of questions, and those in the neighborhood of these questions. If you understand this, there's no reason to get worked up over definitions.

The Confusion

A significant source of confusion for many people who think of ethics as subjective is failing to distinguish between people's *beliefs* about ethics—what they believe to be ethically right or wrong, good or bad, and so on—and ethics itself. And in running these two things together, they make misguided claims about the subjectivity of ethics when they're really making claims about the variance of people's beliefs. To see this, let's take a step back.

There's our belief about whether the earth is flat or round, on the one hand, and there's the actual shape of the earth, on the other. There's our belief about the chemical composition of water being H_2O or H_3O, on the one hand, and there's the actual chemical composition of water, on the other. There's our belief about whether the 2020 election was stolen or legitimate, on the one hand, and there's the actual legitimacy of the election, on the other.

We generally distinguish between our beliefs about X and what X is actually like, and sometimes our beliefs are true, and sometimes they are false. If we didn't make this distinction between our beliefs about X, on the one hand, and what X is actually like, on the other, then we'd have to think that believing X makes it so, but no one thinks that believing the earth is spherical or flat, that water is H_3O or H_2O, or that the election was stolen or legitimate makes the earth spherical, or water composed of H_2O, or the election legitimate.

Of course, people's beliefs about these can change or evolve over time. At one point, most people believed that the earth is flat, they didn't believe that water is H_2O (in their defense, they didn't know anything about chemistry), and some people changed from believing the election was stolen to believing it was legitimate. So, our beliefs change about these things, but the things they had (or didn't have) beliefs about were what they were all along. It's not as though the earth changed from being flat to spherical.

Let's keep going with this distinction: there's our belief about the ethical permissibility or impermissibility of slavery, on the one hand, and there's whether slavery is ethically permissible, on the other. If anything is ethically *impermissible*, it's slavery.

At one point, most people—particularly those who benefited from slavery—believed that slavery was ethically permissible. But people's beliefs changed or evolved over time, and now all believe slavery is wrong. The wrongness of slavery didn't change; it was always wrong. (Quick note: there's a separate issue about the extent to which those who thought it was ethically permissible are deserving of *blame*, given that everyone around them also thought it was permissible, but we won't discuss that here.)

In a way, all this is fairly obvious. *Of course* there's a difference between what people believe about X and what X is actually like. But things tend to get very weird when people talk about ethics; the distinction goes right out the window. People will say things like, "Your ethics is different from my ethics" or "Ethics is subjective because ethics or morality varies across cultures and individuals," or "Ethics has evolved over time; people once thought slavery was ethically permissible and now they think it's not."

But now we can see that "your ethics is different from my ethics" can mean either "what's ethically right for you is ethically wrong for me" or "what you believe is ethically right is something I believe is ethically wrong." And we've already seen that while its clear ethical beliefs change or evolve over time, that doesn't mean that what is right or wrong changes over time. What's weird is that, when people say these things, they are often thinking of ethical beliefs as *the same thing as* ethical right and wrong, and that's just confusion.

The question about whether ethics is subjective is, to be clear, not a question about whether people's ethical beliefs vary over time and across individuals and cultures. Of course they do! The question about whether ethics is subjective is about whether what's right or wrong, or good or bad, varies across time, individuals, and cultures. Now that we understand that, we can look at common reasons for thinking that ethics is subjective.

Three Really Bad Reasons for Thinking Ethics Is Subjective

To say ethics is subjective is to say that there are no facts about what is ethically right, wrong, good, bad, permissible, impermissible, and so on. If ethics is subjective, then not only do ethical *beliefs* vary by individual and culture, but *ethics itself* varies by individual and culture. If ethics is subjective, then there's no such thing as *responsible* ethical inquiry because no one can possibly be incorrect in their conclusions (and so much for responsible AI ethics, or "responsible AI"). If ethics is subjective, then it's touchy-feely, squishy, fuzzy, and not a subject for serious people and certainly not for serious people in a business context.

Now we know what ethics is about. And we know to distinguish between ethical beliefs about what is right or wrong and what *is* right or wrong. But even people who know these things can still think ethics is subjective. And in those nearly twenty years of teaching philosophy, I've noticed three primary reasons for the belief that ethics is subjective, each of which is flatly misguided. I'll lay out the reasons and then explain what's wrong with them. And to be clear: this is not just my view that these are bad reasons. Philosophers don't agree about a lot, but there's a consensus that even if ethics is subjective, it's not for any of these reasons.

Really Bad Reason #1: Ethics is subjective because people disagree about what's right and wrong. People engage in ethical disputes; they disagree about whether abortion and capital punishment are morally permissible, whether you should lie to the police to protect your friend, and whether collecting people's data without their knowledge in exchange for the otherwise free use of your services is ethically permissible. And since there is so much disagreement—so many different moral and ethical beliefs—ethics is subjective; there's *no truth* to the matter.

Really Bad Reason #2: Science delivers us truth. Ethics isn't science, so it doesn't deliver us truth. Science, and more specifically, the scientific method, is *the only* way we discover truths about the world. Empirical observations ("seeing is believing") and investigations (scientific experiments, for instance) deliver facts about the world. Everything else is interpretation, which is to say, subjective. Again, ethics is subjective because empirical observations have a monopoly on truth; ethics and ethical inquiry, because it is not empirical inquiry, concerns the realm of nontruth. In short: *only scientifically verifiable claims are true.*

Really Bad Reason #3: Ethics requires an authority figure to say what's right and wrong; otherwise, it's subjective. You have your beliefs and I have mine and that other person has theirs. And it's not like we have scientific evidence that one view is right and another is wrong, so who's to say what's right and what's wrong? It's all subjective. Or in short: *if there are ethical truths, then there must be an authority figure who makes this right and that wrong.*

What's So Bad about the Bad Reasons

Why Really Bad Reason #1 is really bad. The first reason for thinking ethics is subjective is that people disagree about what is right or wrong, and if people disagree about that stuff, then there's no truth to the matter. Is this a good argument? You guessed it . . . it's really bad! And you can see how bad it is when you consider the following principle:

If people disagree about X, then there's
no truth to the matter about X.

Now that principle is obviously false. People disagree about all sorts of things about which there's a truth to the matter. People disagree about whether humans are the product of evolution, whether self-driving cars will replace human-driven cars within a decade, whether there's something at the center of a black hole, and even whether the earth is flat or spherical. But no one thinks, "Well, guess there's no truth to the matter about the shape of the earth!"

The fact that people disagree about X doesn't show that there's no truth to the matter about X.

And so, too, with ethics. The fact that people disagree about whether lying to protect your friend from the police, whether people should own their data, whether Facebook engages in ethically unacceptable manipulation of its users, and so on, doesn't show that there's no truth to the matter about those issues.

"But," people retort, "it's different with ethics. That's an exception to the principle."

But why should we think it's different with ethics? Why should we think it's exempt from the lesson we just learned about disagreement and truth?

The answer is the same 99 percent of the time: "Because in those other cases of disagreement, they can be scientifically settled. With ethics, there's no way to scientifically settle it."

That's a fine reply, in a way. But it's really an *abandonment* of the first reason for thinking ethics is subjective and a retreat to Really Bad Reason #2 for thinking ethics is subjective. The reply just says, "Only scientifically verifiable claims are true." So let's investigate that.

Why Really Bad Reason #2 is really bad. This one is surprisingly easy to refute. It says only scientifically verifiable claims are true. Actually, let's really throw this into high relief:

Claim: Only scientifically verifiable claims are true.

If you're particularly astute, you just asked yourself a question: "If this is a claim, and the claim says that only scientifically verifiable claims are true, what about this claim?"

This question reveals the problem with the position: it's self-undermining. After all, how would you scientifically verify this claim? Give it to the chemist, or the biologist, or the physicist, or the geologist, and say, "Please perform an experiment to verify this claim." What could they possibly do? Write it on a piece of paper and measure how much weight the paper has gained? Attach it to a seismic reader? Put some cells on it? There's just nothing for them to do, and that's because the claim is not itself scientifically verifiable. So, anyone who believes the claim would, if they are to be consistent, have to stop believing it. And for those who never believed it in the first place, they're fine. So, whatever you do, don't believe the claim. It's false.

Why Really Bad Reason #3 is really bad. OK, almost there. You might think that for ethics not to be subjective, there have to be ethical facts, and for there to be ethical facts, there will have to be an authority figure to say what's right and wrong.

But this is to ignore some basic ways we think about facts. No one says that if there are going to be facts about the shape of the earth, or the evolutionary history of humans, or the chemical composition of water, then there must be an authority figure that makes these things facts. Instead, there are facts about these things and there are people (scientists, of course) who give us the *evidence* for the claims that the earth is spherical, humans are the product of biological evolution, and water is composed of H_2O. It's the evidence, the arguments they offer us for those conclusions, that wins the day, and it's certainly not the *discoverers* of that evidence that make the earth spherical or water composed of H_2O.

If there are moral or ethical facts, then we should expect them to act the same way as other facts. There is no need for an authority figure to make them true. Instead, there are people (philosophers and theologians, for instance) who give evidence or arguments for the ethical claims they make. Think of the many arguments, counterarguments, and counters to the counterarguments in discussions of the moral permissibility of abortion. None of these people say, "I think it's wrong, so it's wrong." If they did, we'd pay them no attention. When we're at our best, we pay attention to their arguments and investigate whether they're sound, just as we do with scientific arguments.

Why This Matters

It's important we get rid of these confusions and bad arguments. In ethics, including in areas related to artificial intelligence, we face very real ethical problems. Those problems, if not properly solved both ethically and technically, can lead to disastrous consequences. But if we give up on ethics as being something objective, as something we can reason about and give arguments for and reasonably change our minds about, then we give up ethical inquiry being a tool at our disposal to solve these real problems.

Let me get a little more specific. I've witnessed hundreds if not thousands of discussions on issues of ethical import. And they all go the same way, so long as people feel comfortable to air their views. You get some people arguing for one side, others arguing for others, and the ones who are not sure where they stand. This is difficult stuff. And then someone says, "I mean, what does it matter? This is all subjective anyway." And then everyone looks at each other, blinks, and shrugs. End of discussion. Every. Time.

Until I ask, "Why do you think ethics is subjective?" Without fail, I get the Really Bad Reasons. Once we've dismantled them, people take up the issue again, this time invulnerable to a comment that would lead them completely off the rails.

You do not need to start your AI ethics program with talking about the nature of ethics. But if you do not involve it at some point, I promise you—I *promise you*—people are going to bring up the Really Bad Reasons. And then you'll have a bunch of people who resent political correctness or touchy-feely stuff standing in the way of technological greatness. You'll also get reduced compliance with your AI ethics program and increased risk. What people think about AI ethics is going to play a role in whether you have an effective AI ethics program.

C'mon . . . Ethics? . . . Objective?

I'm not *really* trying to convince you that ethics is not subjective. I'm not trying to convince you that there are ethical facts. I am trying to convince you that the standard reasons for thinking ethics is subjective are really bad reasons, and failure to see this can lead to a lot of trouble. But the fact that there are three really bad reasons for thinking ethics is subjective doesn't mean that there can't be a fourth reason for thinking ethics is subjective that is really good.

We're not going to go there in this book. The point of defusing those really bad reasons is that they continually put a stop to fruitful discussions and are an impediment to genuine organizational buy-in, from the top to the bottom. Ninety-nine percent of people who see why they're really bad reasons are ready to accept that ethics isn't subjective, and so the practical aim of discussing this is accomplished.

For those of you who are not convinced, however, you should at least think that thinking that there are ethical facts is not an unreasonable position. It's certainly not *crazy*. And so, *for the purposes of creating and participating in an AI ethical risk program*, I hereby invite you to join those people in practice. It will enable you to think about what an effective system for identifying and mitigating those risks would look like. It will enable you to have reason- or evidence-based conversations with colleagues about what is the right thing to do. And it will ensure you don't unhelpfully shut down important conversations that lead to the protection of your organization from ethical, reputational, regulatory, and legal risks.

Why Not Just Talk about Consumer Perception Instead of Ethics?

You might be wondering why we need to talk about ethics at all. Why not just talk about consumer ethical beliefs or consumer perception more generally? Then you can do your standard market research and simply make those your ethical standards internally. AI ethics is really just brand values built into AI product development and deployment, so let's put all this ethics talk to the side. In fact, let's drop this "AI Ethics" label and call it what it is: "AI Consumer Perceptions."

This is an entirely reasonable question. I do not think it rests on confusion or misunderstanding or naivete or an ethical character flaw. It's not a *crazy* thing to do. That said, it's unwise. Here are three reasons why I advise against it.

Lucy, you have some operationalizing to do . . . Adopting your consumers' or clients' ethical views still gives you an ethical view that you now have to operationalize. The problem is that the relatively coarse-grained analyses of customer perception are not well suited to answer the fine-grained decisions you'll need to make. For instance, everyone of minimal moral decency—including your consumers, of course—opposes discriminating against people on the basis of race. But how you should think about discrimination in the context of, say, determining which metrics to use for evaluating whether your model outputs are discriminatory is not something consumers can help you with. Here the issue is actually twofold: first, your customers' ethical perceptions are too coarse-grained to easily transfer to your fine-grained problems, and second, your problems are ones that your customers haven't even thought about yet.

Facebook, for instance, is under a lot of scrutiny for the way its algorithms determine what content to serve up in people's news feeds. A popular documentary, *The Social Dilemma*, has been made about the issue. But when Facebook engineers and product developers were writing those algorithms, they couldn't even begin to ask their customers what they thought because their customers don't understand anything about algorithms, the potential pitfalls, what data is being collected and what's being done with it, and so on. So Facebook—and any company engaged in producing innovative technologies—needs to anticipate the ways various ethical risks might be realized in advance of its customers knowing that these technologies exist and thus in advance of them having any ethical beliefs or perceptions to detect in the first place.

Trust requires ethical leadership. Companies require consumers to trust them if they are to attract and maintain those consumers, and nothing violates trust quite as mercilessly as an ethics breach at scale. Think #DeleteFacebook, #DeleteUber, #BoycottStarbucks. Each of those companies violated consumer trust—trust that they would protect your data, trust that they would treat their workers respectfully, and trust that they would ensure a nondiscriminatory environment for African Americans, respectively—that led to going viral for all the wrong reasons. The vaccine is ethical leadership.

I don't mean that corporations need to be Gandhi. I mean they need to articulate their ethical values clearly and explain how they live up to them. If a company can't do that, but instead simply mouths fealty to an ethical code and then runs to market research on consumer sentiments of the day and makes decisions solely on the basis of that, it can expect its ethics messaging to justifiably ring hollow and thereby lose the trust of its consumers. Just think about how much time you want to spend with the person who espouses various values and then does whatever the cool kids tell them to do.

Organizational buy-in. I've stressed that creating an AI ethics program requires buy-in from the top to the bottom, and an anathema to that buy-in is for employees to see AI ethics as PR or bowing to political correctness. If your general AI ethics strategy just reduces to a strategy of deferring to consumer survey results, you should expect that you won't only fail to get buy-in from a great variety of internal stakeholders, but also that you'll alienate the growing number of employees who are passionate about AI ethics and will accuse you of ethics washing. If you want buy-in, you're going to have to take ethics, not just ethical perceptions of your consumers, very seriously.

Where We Go Next

The foundations of ethics, now concrete, are settled. It's time to build on that foundation by understanding bias, explainability, and privacy concerns in a way that reveals what Structure we need. We'll start in the next chapter with the most contentious issue of all: discriminatory AI.

Recap

- Putting an AI ethics program into practice requires getting organizational buy-in. Getting that buy-in requires that people understand what AI ethics is. Understanding what AI ethics is requires understanding something about AI and something about ethics.
- Major stumbling blocks for understanding crucial aspects of what ethics is include confusing ethical beliefs with ethical facts and the Really Bad Reasons that lead people to think and talk about ethics as being "squishy" or "subjective." Thinking about ethics in this way is to think that there are no ethical facts to be discovered, and this ultimately leads people to shrug their shoulders when it comes to thinking carefully about identifying and mitigating ethical risks.
- AI ethics should not be reduced to reactions to market research on consumer perception or sentiment, for at least three reasons: (1) an AI ethics program involves operationalizing a set of values, which consumer perception reports are silent on, (2) consumers are looking for ethical leadership, and a mere appeal to the sentiment of the day does not meet that bar, and (3) that approach will alienate both those who are not particularly concerned about the ethical risks of AI within your organization and those who are, leading to a lack of compliance and turnover, respectively.
- All of this means you'll need to provide your people with education about both AI and ethics.

2

Bias

In Search of Fair AI

Person 1 and a friend were in a rush to pick up a child from school on time. In a foolish scheme to get there faster, they attempted to steal a bike and a scooter. Combined, the scooter and bike were worth $80, and both belonged to a six-year-old, whose mother saw the two people and yelled after them. Realizing this, the two quickly dropped the vehicles and ran off. Person 1 had previously been charged with four juvenile misdemeanors.

In another case, Person 2 stole tools from a hardware store worth $86.35. Previously, Person 2 had spent five years in prison for armed robbery and attempted armed robbery and was charged a third time for attempted armed robbery.

Suppose you're a judge and you had to determine the risk of Person 1 or Person 2 committing a crime (not a misdemeanor) in the next two years. As for myself, if I were the judge, I would be harsher with Person 2 than Person 1. That's because it looks to me like Person 1 is a much lower risk than Person 2; juvenile misdemeanors are not the kinds of red flags that multiple cases of armed robbery are.

The judge in this case disagreed with me. Not only did the judge rate Person 1 as a higher risk than Person 2, but the judge also rated Person 1 an eight out of ten risk and Person 2 a three out of ten.

Three more important facts about this case:

- Person 1 is a young Black woman.
- Person 2 is a middle-aged white man.
- The judge who determined the risk scores was an AI software.

The case is not isolated. As a landmark 2016 piece by ProPublica reported about this software, called COMPAS: holding fixed prior crime records and types of crime, Black defendants were predicted to be 77 percent more likely to commit a violent crime and 45 percent more likely to commit a crime of any kind.[1]

Again, that's *holding fixed* all other variables. You simply cannot talk about how to approach the content of an AI ethical risk program without seriously talking about biased AI, and there is *a lot* of talk about it.

Viable solutions, on the other hand, are hard to come by, and current approaches leave a lot of risk on the table.

The State of the Art

At the highest level, ML takes a set of inputs, performs various calculations, and creates a set of outputs. For instance, input this data about loan applicants, and output data about who is approved or denied. Input data about what transactions occurred where, when, and by whom, and output data about whether the transactions are legitimate or fraudulent. Or input criminal justice histories, résumés, and symptoms, and get outputs relating to criminal risk, interview worthiness, and diseases, respectively.

One thing ML is doing here is distributing goods and services: loans, interviews, housing, and so on. And *if* you have information about the demographics of your applicants—more on this later—then you can see how those approvals or denials are distributed across the various subpopulations. We might see, for instance, that this résumé-reading AI, which was trained on the hiring data of the past ten years within the organization that built the AI, looks like this:

- Interviews 30 percent of all men who apply
- Interviews 20 percent of all women who apply
- Interviews 10 percent of all Black men who apply
- Interviews 5 percent of all Black women who apply

That looks, on the face of it, fairly suspicious. It sure looks a lot like this AI is biased against women, Black men, and Black women especially.

What we've done, presumably, is identified that the ML is biased or discriminatory. But how can we know for sure? What constitutes a discriminatory set of outputs? Can we quantify it? Can we devise software that will check for biased outputs that also *measures* that bias?

That's exactly what a variety of big tech companies, startups, and nonprofits have created, and they've done so by making use of various metrics and "definitions" of fairness and bias as found in the academic research on machine learning fairness.

Things get very technical very quickly, but we don't need to dive into those details. All we need to know is that there are various quantitative metrics for fairness against which the outputs of various ML models can be compared. And identifying bias in this way also lends itself to mitigating the bias, that is, to choosing a bias-mitigation strategy. Engineers and data scientists need to tweak the product in such a way that it does better according to the metrics, resulting in less biased outputs and so the right "decisions" being made about who should or should not get a loan, an interview, housing, and so on.

But rejoicing would be a bit too quick. There are at least five problems with this approach.

First, there are roughly two dozen quantitative metrics for fairness, and crucially, they are *not compatible with each other.*[2] You simply cannot be fair according to all of them at the same time.

For example, Northpointe, the maker of the COMPAS software that provides risk ratings on defendants referenced in the opening of this chapter, replied to charges of discrimination by pointing out that it was using a different and perfectly legitimate quantitative metric for fairness. More specifically, COMPAS aimed to maximize its true positive rate across Black and white defendants. The idea behind it is fairly simple: it's really bad to let people who are likely to reoffend go free. The better we are at identifying those people, the better we do.

ProPublica used a different metric for fairness: the rate of false positives across white and Black defendants. The idea behind this is fairly simple as well: it's really bad to jail people who are unlikely to reoffend. The better we are at not unnecessarily jailing people, the better we do.

So Northpointe wanted to maximize true positives, while ProPublica wanted to minimize false positives. Crucially, you can't do both at once. When you maximize true positives, you increase false positives, and when you minimize false positives, you decrease true positives.

The technical tools for bias identification and mitigation cannot help here. They can tell you how your various tweaks to your AI result in different scores according to these different fairness metrics, but they simply cannot tell you which metric to use. In other words, they leave a lot of the ethical risk on the table.

That means that an *ethical* judgment needs to be made for which data scientists and engineers are ill-equipped: Which, if any, of these quantitative metrics of fairness are the ethical or appropriate ones to use? That these technicians are ill-equipped has nothing to do with their respective characters, but rather that they simply have not received the education and training in grappling with complex ethical dilemmas. In short, when it comes to making these kinds of judgments, the experts are not in the room: not lawyers, and certainly not political theorists or ethicists. But if the experts aren't in the room, you cannot expect an expert decision. Failing to take this into account can have real-world consequences.

This brings us to our first "Structure from Content Lesson." I'll highlight these each time our understanding of the Content side of things—for example, that bias and discrimination are ethically complex issues that cannot be solved for with a technical or mathematical fix—reveals to us that we need something in our Structure:

> **Structure from Content Lesson #1:** There must be an individual or, better, a set of individuals with relevant ethical, legal, and business expertise, who determine which, if any,

of the mathematical metrics of fairness are appropriate for the particular use case.[3]

The "if appropriate" qualification in this lesson is important and speaks to a question virtually all of my clients ask me: "Are all differential distributions of a good across subpopulations unfair? Aren't we sometimes justified in distributing [loans, ads, recommendations, etc.] differently across groups?"

In short, the answer is yes. First, there are cases in which the good or service being distributed is not exactly crucial to living a decent life. Suppose, for instance, your AI recommends what film to watch next, and it turns out that recommendations for Steven Spielberg films are differentially distributed across various subpopulations. This is hardly the kind of issue we need to worry about in the context of discriminatory models. Second, there are plausible cases in which some subpopulations do receive a piece of the pie that is outsized given their representation in the population at large, but we don't think that must be stopped on pain of being unjust. For instance, and to take a somewhat controversial example, people of Asian descent and Jewish people are disproportionately granted entry to elite universities and colleges. At the very least, it's not at all obvious this needs to be "corrected for" by applying quantitative metrics of fairness. This is all just to say that there are cases and cases and cases, and as Structure from Lesson #1 says, you need the appropriate people in place to determine which, if any, of the quantitative metrics for fairness are appropriate given your use case.

Second, these tools don't recommend bias-mitigation *strategies* once bias has been identified, and there is no one-size-fits-all solution. Take, for instance, facial-recognition software that is biased against Black women (by virtue of being worse at identifying them than at other subpopulations), and the hiring software imagined at the start of this chapter, which is also biased against Black women.

In the case of facial-recognition software, the problem lies with under-sampling—with not getting enough data.[4] The training data set simply didn't include enough pictures of Black women (from different angles, different lighting conditions, etc.). The bias-mitigation strategy, in broad strokes, is clear: go get more pictures of Black women. (I say "in broad strokes" since how, exactly, one goes about getting those pictures, and doing so in an ethical way, is another matter.)

In the case of the software that rated the hirees' risk, the bias is the result of noticing a certain pattern in the historical data pertaining to hires made within the organization, specifically, "we don't hire women around here." In this case, getting *more* data—diving into the last twenty years instead of just the last ten years of hiring data, say—would be a terrible bias-mitigation strategy. In fact, it would only serve to entrench the existing bias.

How, exactly, to determine the range of bias-mitigation strategies on the menu and then which strategy to deploy in a particular use case is a complicated matter, involving ethical, legal, and business risks. These technical tools cannot (and should not) make those kinds of decisions. And so we arrive at . . .

> **Structure from Content Lesson #2:** You need an individual or, ideally, set of individuals, who have the relevant expertise for choosing appropriate bias-mitigation strategies.

Third, these tools measure the outputs of AI models, which is to say that bias identification occurs well into the development life cycle: it occurs after data sets have been chosen and models have been trained, which is to say, after a good deal of resources have been devoted to the product. It is then inefficient, not to mention unpopular, to go back to the drawing board if a bias problem is detected that cannot be solved in a way that involves relatively minimal tweaking of the AI. The probability of bias being mitigated from step one of product development is greatly increased, as is the efficiency of bias mitigation, when attempts at bias identification begin before training the model, for instance, during training data collection. Further, choosing the relevant fairness metrics before training your model protects you from choosing metrics that you test well against already; it is no great feat to score well on fairness metrics when you simply choose the subset of metrics you're already scoring well on. And so we come to another Structure from Content Lesson.

> **Structure from Content Lesson #3:** Attempts at identifying and mitigating potential biases of your models should start before training your model and, ideally, before determining what your training data sets should look like and be sourced from. (In fact, the probability of avoiding creating a discriminatory AI should be taken into account before deciding to build an AI solution in the first place.)

Fourth, these technical tools do not cover all types of bias. They do not, for instance, ferret out whether your search engine has labeled Black people "gorillas."[5] It does not check whether your chatbot is being culturally insensitive to, say, people in Japan by failing to use language that is commensurate with a culture that honors its elders. These are cases of bias, or in the latter case, cultural insensitivity, for which no technical tool exists. Some people call these "representational harms," as opposed to the "allocative" harms of an unjust distribution of goods or services.

Fifth, the ways these tools measure for bias are arguably *not* compatible with existing antidiscrimination law.[6] Antidiscrimination law forbids companies from using variables like race and gender in their decision-making processes. But what if using those variables is necessary to test AI models for bias and thus influences the changes AI teams make to the model in an effort to mitigate bias? That not only looks ethically permissible, but plausibly ethically required as well. This leaves companies in the awkward position of making an important and substantive decision that may reasonably vary on a case-by-case basis: whether they should mitigate the biases of their model in a way that (antiquated) antidiscrimination law forbids or instead whether they should act in accordance with existing antidiscrimination law and either push out a biased model or cancel the project altogether.

> **Structure from Content Lesson #4:** You should include a lawyer when determining the appropriate bias-mitigation techniques.

Where Does the Potential for Discrimination Come From?

The five problems with current technical approaches to bias mitigation don't arise because it's difficult to identify processes or oversight structures. They arise because there are Content-related risks at play. Which, if any, of the various mathematical "definitions" of fairness is the *appropriate* metric to use in this use case? "Appropriate" in this context refers to ethical, reputational, regulatory, legal, and business risks. Are there ways the model can be unfair or unjust in a way that isn't captured by these metrics? Are all differential impacts on various subpopulations discriminatory or is it sometimes permissible or even required?

The overarching question in this context that an organization needs to ask is: Can the outputs of our models lead to discriminatory outputs and, if so, what do we do about it? At the risk of repeating myself, I'll say it again: *this is a Content issue, not a Structure issue*. Who should ask that question, when they should ask it, what they should do when they're not sure . . . those are all issues pertaining to Structure. And the clearer we get on the Content issues, the easier and more successful we'll be at building a Structure.

It's impossible to list all the possible ways a discriminatory AI can be created. There are just too many. But here are six common examples in two categories.

Category One: Problems with Your Training Data

Example one: Real-world discrimination. The world can be an ugly place. One way in which it's ugly is that discrimination exists, now and especially throughout history. Now suppose you want to train your AI to approve or disapprove mortgages, and you use historical data about who has been granted mortgages in the past. As it turns out, due to real-world discrimination, Black people are given mortgages at lower percentages, and so your training data reflects that fact. The pattern your AI learns is, "we don't lend to Black people."

Example two: Under-sampling. The world has a lot of complexity, and your training data set may fail to capture all of it. Suppose, for instance, you want data about the travel patterns of people commuting to and from work so that you can schedule public transportation accordingly. Your training data consists of geolocations of smartphones during standard commuting hours. But not everyone can afford a smartphone; usually wealthier people have them (which also correlates with race in the United States). Your training data thus under-samples data concerning the commuting patterns of those financially less well-off. As a result, your AI trains on when wealthier people commute, and so you'll likely make decisions that benefit the neighborhoods in which wealthy people live, resulting in a relative disadvantage for those less well-off.

Example three: Proxy bias. Sometimes you cannot get data about what you actually want data about, so you use a proxy. Suppose you want to create a risk rating AI for criminal defendants, and you want to know the likelihood that someone will commit a crime within two years after being released. But you can't get data about who has committed a crime, so instead you use data about being *accused* of a crime, for example, data about who is arrested. As it turns out, though, certain populations are arrested at higher rates for a variety of reasons, for example, disproportionate policing (which may be related to discriminatory attitudes, a response to relatively increased crime rates, or both). The more you police a population, the more problems you'll see (all else equal), and so the more arrests you'll make, even if those same problems are arising at the same rate in a less-policed population. The result? The software says that Black people are more likely to commit a crime—whoops! I mean to be arrested—than white people.

Category Two: Problems with Testing and How You Think about the Use Case

Example four: Coarse-grained model. People are different, and if you treat them all the same, you may run into problems. Suppose you want to make a diabetes-detecting AI. You actually have good data from different subpopulations, but ultimately your AI applies the same criteria for diagnosis regardless of the patient's particular ethnicity or gender. The problem is that diabetes presents differently across ethnicity and gender, and so failing to take that into consideration leads to misdiagnosis. The one-size-fits-all model simply doesn't work.

Example five: Benchmark or testing bias. You want to test your AI against a benchmark that other (perhaps competitor) AIs are judged against. But suppose the benchmark is biased. Suppose you train your mortgage-lending AI and then see how well it does with the benchmark data set used by most mortgage lenders. And suppose it tests extraordinarily well, at least in one respect: the rate of true positives—the rate at which it correctly identifies people of being mortgage-worthy—is very high. "Success!" you think. Only it turns out that the benchmark data set has itself drastically under-sampled mortgages given to Black people. The result is that you think you have a highly accurate mortgage-worthy predictor, when in fact you have a highly accurate mortgage-worthy-white-person predictor.[7]

Example six: Objective function bias. Your goals themselves can unintentionally lead to disparate impacts among various subpopulations. Suppose you're in the business of determining who should get a lung transplant. One thing you might reasonably think is, "We want to get as many years out of these lungs as we can. We certainly don't want to give the lungs to a ninety-year-old who will only get a bit of use out of them when we can give them to an eighteen-year-old instead." So, you use your AI to determine which patients are most likely to use the lungs for the greatest length of time. As it turns out, Black people tend not to live as long as white people, so you've inadvertently favored white people over Black people in the distribution of lung transplants into your AI model.

This is a particularly contentious case. One might reply, "Look, the ethically best option is to maximize years saved. We, as a health-care company, can't take into account various complicated historical injustices or even happenstance. It's simply not within our purview or responsibilities, and frankly, we don't have the resources to carry out the kind of investigation that we would have to in order to make a well-informed decision about our role vis-à-vis racial justice."

Then again, one might also say, "We are a health-care company, and we cannot undo all historical injustices. But insofar as we can either further aggravate those injustices or play a role in evening the playing field, we should do the latter, and this is one place where we can ensure that the Black population has as much access to life-saving treatments as any other population. If that means making some other ethical sacrifice, like not maximizing years saved, at least in the short term, then so be it."

This is a *very* difficult Content issue. To answer it—or any other question in which determining an objective function is potentially discriminatory—an organization will have to dig deeper into the issue. As for *how* to do that, well that *is* a question about Structure.

Mitigation Strategies

Spotting these sources of bias (and others) is not an easy task. What's more, it's only the beginning, since then your team needs to choose an appropriate bias-mitigation strategy. Some strategies will involve getting more data (in the case of under-sampling), getting better proxies or the real thing if you can (in the case of proxy bias), or being very careful about whether your one-size-fits-all model is the right one to be deployed on this population of varying sizes. But wait, there's more!

Decisions are made about how to weight the various inputs to your AI. For instance, when determining the insurance premium for car insurance, you might weigh driving history as more important than age, or type of car as more important than color of car, and so on. If you want different outputs, one way to get there is by altering either which inputs you input or the weights of those inputs. Perhaps, for instance, making zip code count, but not as much, will stop you from discriminating against race, given that zip code often highly correlates with race.

There are also decisions about where you set your thresholds for different populations. AI can output a binary "decision": interview or don't interview, grant or deny loan, serve or don't serve ad, and so on. The predictions or outputs of the AI, though, are often not binary but exist across a spectrum. You'll have to decide where that sharp line should be drawn, that is, what threshold someone has to meet in order to get a yes instead of a no. What should that threshold be? Should you vary the threshold depending on what subpopulation you're making a decision about?

Finally, there are decisions about what to do when you lack the demographic data against which you can compare your outputs.

So far, we've been assuming that your organization has the demographic data of the people that AI will make predictions about. But you may lack that data, and in some cases, it may be illegal for you to ask for that data in the first place. Are there still strategies available for mitigating bias? Perhaps it would be ethically permissible to use proxies for various subpopulations and then attempt a fair distribution across those proxy groups. That, of course, is potentially ethically problematic, not to mention legally questionable.

This is a lot, I know, so let's break it down.

Before you start training your AI:

1. Analyze your training data sets and objective function as potential sources of discriminatory outputs given your use case.
2. Consider whether you might introduce discriminatory outputs by virtue of how you plan on testing your model.
3. Once potential sources of discriminatory outputs have been identified, determine appropriate bias-mitigation strategies for each potential source.
    a. This can include, for instance, getting more data, introducing synthetic (i.e., data scientist–created) data, and changing your objective function.
4. Choose the quantitative metrics of fairness that are appropriate for your intended use case.

After you've trained your AI:

5. Identify whether the AI's outputs are fair by the lights of the fairness metrics you chose before training. If yes, all else equal, proceed to GO and take $200 from the till. If no, proceed to 6.

6. Identify appropriate bias-mitigation strategies. These may include not only those referenced in 3a, above, but also modifying your threshold(s) and adjusting your weightings.

7. Go back to 5.

These instructions are at a fairly high level. They tell you to analyze, consider, and choose. The issues you need to analyze, consider, and choose range from quantitative analyses of data sets to qualitative assessments of what's ethically appropriate to qualitative decisions about appropriate bias-mitigation strategies, which can be constrained not only by the availability of data but also by limited time and resources. In my language, these instructions are at the Content level. *How* you analyze, consider, and choose is a Structure issue. But now you know what your Structure needs to accomplish: it needs to be made in such a way that, among other things, it can systematically, comprehensively, and responsibly analyze, consider, and choose on these kinds of issues, as the Structure from Content Lessons urge. In chapter 6, we'll get into the details of how to build this Structure.

Two Glaring Omissions

Go to any event where AI ethics is discussed and you'll hear at least two passionate appeals to diversity and inclusion as they bear on issues of bias in AI. It's almost cliché at this point to hear, "We need more diversity among our engineers and data scientists developing the AI." Or, "We need to engage stakeholders and get them involved in the design process, especially when the stakeholders are members of historically marginalized populations." We cannot wrap up a conversation about bias in AI without addressing these issues.

The first claim is that we need to have more diverse engineering and product design teams. If we did, that would change how products are made in a way that reflects the demographic diversity of the team. One common example appealed to in the course of this argument is seat-belt design. Seat belts were designed by men, and crash test dummies bear the weights and proportions of the average American male. The result is a worse fit and so greater risk for women, especially pregnant women. Another example is the "racist soap dispenser," which dispenses soap when it senses that a hand is in front of its sensor. The team members who built it were white, and since it only trained on their hands and the light contrast between their hands and the background, it did not dispense soap to people with darker skin.

The second claim is that we need to engage a wider array of stakeholders, particularly members of historically marginalized groups. Examples here that cite particular AI products that would have done better are not so common, though other kinds of examples are aplenty, for instance, policies that disproportionately affect people of color and ad campaigns that insult various communities.

I can generally be described as someone who is an ally and a strong supporter of social justice issues generally and racial justice issues in particular. I think we need to do better as a society, as businesses, and as individuals. I think we need widespread and strategic approaches within businesses to combat various biases in hiring and promotion. All this is to preface that, while talk of diverse engineering teams and consulting stakeholders might feel really good, and those who trumpet it are unquestionably *right* that these things are important for the sake of Justice, there is little evidence that these are the most effective or quickest way to AI bias mitigation. In a way, this is good news, since diversifying engineering and product teams in a way that reflects the diversity of, say, the United States, is a multigenerational goal. If achieving a multigenerational goal is absolutely necessary for identifying and mitigating bias in AI, we're in really big trouble.

A similar issue arises with regard to engaging stakeholders, which no one can reasonably deny is a good idea. Aside from the logistical issues to which it gives rise, it does not by itself mitigate any ethical risks; it leaves them right in place, unless one knows how to think through stakeholder feedback. For instance, suppose your stakeholders are racist. Suppose the norms that are local to where you will deploy your AI encourage gender discrimination. Suppose your stakeholders disagree with each other because, in part, they have conflicting interests; stakeholders are not a monolithic group with a single perspective, after all. Stakeholder input is valuable, and responsible decision-making involves it. But you cannot programmatically derive an ethical decision just from stakeholder input. Whether you defer to or defy (some subset of) stakeholder input, it's a qualitative ethical decision.

Again, having diverse teams and consulting stakeholders is important and it ought to be done. But as a recent paper out of Columbia University found, they are not necessarily the most effective bias-identification and mitigation strategies.[8] It's more important, in the context of talking about bias mitigation in AI, that there exists expertise with regard to the ethical and legal risks that arise when training and testing your model.

What's in the Box?

No one wants discriminatory AI. It's obviously a bad thing. Black boxes, on the other hand, are a bit of a mixed bag, as we'll see in the next chapter.

Recap

- The four Structure from Content Lessons that relate to bias and can guide approaches to Structure that are gleaned from understanding Content are:
    1. There must be an individual or, better, a set of individuals with relevant ethical, legal, or business expertise that determines which, if any, of the mathematical metrics of fairness are appropriate for the particular use case at hand.
    2. You need an individual or, ideally, set of individuals, who have the relevant expertise for choosing appropriate bias-mitigation strategies.
    3. Attempts at identifying and mitigating potential biases of your models should start before training your model and, ideally, before determining what your training data sets should look like and be sourced from.
    4. You should include a lawyer when determining the appropriate bias-mitigation techniques.
- Biased or discriminatory output can arise in a number of ways, including:
    - Real-world discrimination
    - Under-sampling
    - Proxy bias
    - Coarse-grained models
    - Benchmark bias
    - Objective function bias

- Those sources of bias suggest various bias-mitigation strategies, including getting more data, choosing better proxies, using fine-grained data, and determining a different objective function. Other strategies include:
  - Adjusting the weights of inputs
  - Adjusting thresholds for outputs
  - Determining what to do in the light of an absence of demographic data
- Current approaches, including using software that measures outputs against various quantitative metrics of fairness, are inadequate. Their problems include:
  - The metrics are incompatible.
  - They do not address the issue of what bias-mitigation strategy to implement.
  - They address bias too late in the development process.
  - They don't cover all forms of bias.
  - They are potentially incompatible with current antidiscrimination law.
- You should work toward having diverse engineering and product development teams (not to mention a diverse array of senior AI leaders). But that should not be your primary bias-identification and mitigation strategy, both for reasons of effectiveness and speed.

3

Explainability

The Space between the Inputs and the Outputs

You just found the house of your dreams and you go to the bank for a mortgage. You sit down with the loan officer and fill out the application with the requested information: name, date of birth, employment history. You also provide credit card statements, paycheck stubs, details about your investment portfolio, and so on. He takes that stack of paper and puts it into one end of a machine that resembles a photocopier. It rapidly sucks up the paper, whirrs for a bit, and then prints out a single page that just reads: *Nope.*

"I'm sorry, but your request for a mortgage has been denied," the loan officer informs you.

Your excitement crashes to sadness and confusion. "Why?" you ask.

"Because the Machine said so," the officer replies. And when you press for more, he tells you, "We inputted all that data you gave us. The Machine compared all that data against the data of others who have been approved and denied and whether they defaulted or repaid the loan, and apparently your data resembles those who default."

At this point, your confusion turns to rage: "I want to know what about my application led to being denied. This is outrageous. . . . I demand an explanation!"

But for all your fury, you've reached a dead end. It's not that the loan officer is refusing to tell you. And it's not that he's refusing to introduce you to someone who can explain it to you. It's that no one *can* explain it. The Machine is a black box: we can't look inside to see how it comes to its outputs.

If this strikes you as an unacceptable state of affairs, then you're not alone, but it's also largely how many ML algorithms operate. Often those who create them can't explain their outputs. More and more people are demanding that ML outputs be *explainable*: that we refuse the black box and require a transparent glass box.

The issue isn't only one of creating frustration in customers, employees, and others. In some cases, giving explanations for decisions is required by regulations, as it is with decisions regarding whether to approve or deny someone a mortgage. Expect this to be the case with more and more decisions driven by AI. You'll want, or need, an explanation for why you denied someone housing, or an interview, or probation, if not for the target of the decision then for their lawyers when you find yourself in the middle of a lawsuit in which the plaintiff alleges that your AI has discriminated against them. And in still other cases, your employees may demand an explanation for why they didn't get promoted or matched with that newly available position. Here, as elsewhere, if lacking an explanation is an ethical risk, it's also a reputational, regulatory, or legal risk.

Standard discussions of explainability in AI are quite narrow. As with bias, the discussion centers on different technical approaches to peering inside the black box, which, it turns out, is quite difficult and, in some cases, arguably impossible. But rather than focus on those technical approaches and before we start slapping "explainable" and "transparent" on every AI ethics statement, thereby forcing everyone at every conference to decry the existence of black boxes, let's take a step back to see the bigger picture. Because, as you'll see, it's not always important that ML outputs be explainable, and it's not always necessary that the explanation has to be about what goes on between the inputs and the outputs.

Breaking Down Explanations

Let's talk about your dashed hopes of buying your dream house. A lot has gone on here.

1. A while back, before the time of automation, a team at the bank created a mortgage application that asked for various pieces of information about applicants, and it created a simple decision tree for determining whether someone should be approved or denied based on that information.
2. That application got updated in various ways by various people over the years.
3. The bank tracks which loan applicants default on their mortgage and which pay it off successfully.
4. After not so long, the bank finds itself with tens of thousands of applications that have been denied or granted, and it knows which paid and which defaulted.

5. Someone decides that it would be a good idea to automate lending decisions by using ML.

6. They decide to use all that historical information they have on hand. They also realize there's other data they can collect that they deem potentially relevant to the application, for example, social media data (about what social media sites you're on, how often you post, how often you comment, whose posts you comment on, etc.).

7. The team chooses a learning algorithm, of which there are many readily available, that it thinks is good for this task.

8. The algorithm is very good at crunching massive troves of data and finding patterns across thousands of data points.

9. The ML spits out for each applicant a probability that they will default on the mortgage, between 0 and 1. For example, a 0.3345 is a tick above a one-third chance of default, a 0.0178 is just under 2 percent and so on.

10. The team decides that anyone with a probability of default that's higher than 3.74 percent should be denied a mortgage; 3.74 percent is the *threshold* for getting approved or denied.

11. An executive approves the AI for deployment.

12. Marvin the loan officer tells you you're denied.

13. Your animal of a lawyer, staring down the perspiring lead engineer in a deposition, demands an explanation for why you were denied a mortgage.

14. Also, you're Black.

As you can probably tell by even this truncated description (we could have added many more decision points along the way that you never think about), there isn't *the* explanation for why you got denied. Or rather, the one BIG explanation consists of myriad events for which there are smaller explanations: Why did those original writers of the loan applications choose the criteria they did? Why was it updated over the years and what issues—problems? opportunities?—arose that justified making those updates? Why did the engineers and data scientists think social media data might be relevant? Why didn't they think other data was relevant, say, the elementary school you went to? Why did they choose the learning algorithm that they did? Why did the model do what it did with those inputs? Why a 3.74 percent threshold? Why not 3.76 percent, or 12.8 percent? On what grounds did the executive approve the AI for deployment? Answers to each of these questions (and more) comprise the BIG explanation for why you got denied.

With all the answers to these questions and more, we now have two more questions:

1. What are people asking for when they ask for explanations of ML outputs?

2. Of all these explanations, which are the important ones?

Interrogating the Black Box

Most of the explanations for why you got denied a mortgage require us to understand why people made the decisions they did. We'll call those *people explanations*.

We know what people explanations look like: "We decided to automate it because we were getting more applications than we had the personnel to handle. We thought social media data might be relevant because we thought it might reveal patterns of behavior that are predictive of loan repayment. We set 3.74 percent as the threshold because of the way the outputs were clustered, combined with knowledge about our company's risk appetite." We can press harder, though, and ask for even more explanation: "Why not just limit how many applications you accept? Why not hire more people to handle the influx of applications? Why take a gamble on social media data being relevant?" And so on.

Machine explanations, on the other hand, are a bit odd. As articulated in number 8, above, what we're asking for is an explanation of how the model arrived at its outputs given the inputs. Actually, there are two questions we should have in mind.

- What are the rules that transform inputs to outputs?
  - You've got a bunch of data as input. Your ML model takes all that data, notices various patterns across that data, and gives an output. For instance, you've trained your ML to know what your dog Pepe looks like in a picture by training it with a thousand photos of your dog. Your ML learned what your dog looks like by analyzing each picture at the pixel level; how pixel #373 is shaded and is situated relative to that pixel and that other one (and thousands of others). Sometimes it stands in this set of relations to those pixels (e.g., when it's sitting) and sometimes it stands in that set of relations to those pixels (e.g., when it's standing). In other words, it learns "rules" that are roughly characterized as "when the pixels look like

this, it's Pepe, and when the pixels don't look like that, it's not Pepe." These kinds of machine explanations are called *global explanations*.

- Why did it yield this particular output given these particular inputs?
  - Why did *you* with your particular data profile get denied a mortgage? Was it the frequency at which you change jobs? Was it that you got charged with the misdemeanor of reckless driving five years ago? Was it that you've taken out too many credit cards? Was it that you posted a lot of comments on that one guy's profile? Machine explanations that answer these kinds of questions are called *local explanations*.

ML is in the business of recognizing complex patterns. So complex, in fact, that they defy human understanding. Think about trying to wrap one's head around the quantity of pixels in a picture and the various mathematical relations they can stand in to other pixels such that you grasp how the rules regarding how to label photos "Pepe" or "Not Pepe" are arrived at, or how this particular inputted photo led the ML to output "This is Pepe"; it's simply not possible.

This is the way in which machine explanations differ from people explanations. We give explanations of people's decisions in a language we can understand. We can grasp the connections those explanations articulate; we understand how the influx of credit applications would lead someone to consider a range of solutions for that problem, including automation. With machine explanations, it's just so complex; both the quantity of variables at play and the quantity of relationships among those variables confound our feeble human minds, even if we do generally grasp the mathematical language in which all of this complexity is communicated.

Now we have a grip on what people are asking for when they ask for explainable AI: people explanations, machine explanations, or both. And when they ask for machine explanations, they're asking for global explanations, local explanations, or both.

You might think that we may as well just have all the explanations all the time. But machine explanations don't come for free, and there are other things you might want to spend your resources on. Most importantly, achieving the goal of an explainable model often comes at the cost of decreased accuracy. That's because, to simplify things a bit, the very same features that increase accuracy also decrease our ability to understand: the complexity of the patterns the ML recognizes. All else equal, the more data you have, the more (intricate) patterns your ML can recognize and so the more accurate it can get. Put differently, all else equal, the more examples you have to learn from, the better. But the more data and the more (intricate) patterns your ML finds, the less likely you are to understand what's going on. Turning up the volume on explainability tends to turn down the volume on accuracy, and vice versa.[1]

This points us to another Structure from Content Lesson.

> **Structure from Content Lesson #5:** You need the right people to determine whether people explanations, global machine explanations, local machine explanations, or all of the above are important for a given use case.

As for what should guide the deliberations of those people—how they should determine which explanations matter and when—that will depend on why explanations are important in the first place.

The Importance of Explanation

You're married. As far as you can see, things are going reasonably well. There's no violence, shared laughter, not infrequent moments of intimacy, and so on. One day, you wake up to find your spouse packing her bags.

"Where are you going?" you ask.

"I'm leaving you. And I'm taking Pepe with me."

"But why?" you protest.

"Nope," she says. And walks out the door, dog in tow.

You're bound to be infuriated. After all, you just moved into your dream house after successfully suing the bank that denied you a mortgage. Now its vast interior mocks your lonely existence.

One thing you'll turn over and over in your head at 3 a.m. in your California king is "Why?" "Why did she leave me?" And you'll want an answer to that question for at least three reasons.

First, it's disrespectful to provide no explanation. You're not some inanimate object to be tossed aside. You're a person of worth, and as such, you're owed an explanation as an expression of the recognition of that worth. Refusing to explain and walking out adds insult to injury.

Second, had you known the explanation, perhaps you could have done something about it. Was it because you're not "present"?

Because you can agree to turn off your phone inside the house and maybe that would help. Was it because you haven't been romantic enough? Because you can give greater attention to that; are there such things as romance coaches? You'll Google it. Or is it because you're stretched too thin with the overhead of a mortgage you can barely afford? Because you can sell the house or, screw it, that bank sucks anyway, you'll default on the mortgage, prove Marvin right, and move to Costa Rica together.

Third, you want to know the general rules for how to live together and think about whether those rules are any good. What are the expectations of you? If you fix this one thing today, will it be another thing tomorrow? "What are the rules here? There's nothing I can do about my mother, so if that's at play here, that just seems really unfair. Or maybe it's not my mother . . . maybe it was all that talk about 'coming from different places.' Was that code for 'you're Black and I'm white' all along?"

Each of these types of concerns can play out in an ML output. If we create an ML that determines whether you get a loan or an interview, see a job ad, get matched with this person on the dating site, and so on, you probably want an explanation because it shows respect, because it helps you understand what you can do to change the outcome, and because you want to determine if the rules you're being asked to play by are fair in the first place. Were you denied that loan because you're Black?

These three reasons for the importance of explainability, however, do not provide us with obvious guidance. Remember: explainable ML outputs are not free. We need to balance its importance against other considerations like accuracy and what resources we have or lack to devote to explainability. In some cases, we might think machine explanations are unnecessary. In others, it's a nice-to-have but not a need-to-have. In still others, it's essential.

As with all such decisions, there is no simple decision tree for determining how important explainability will be in each use case. However, armed with an understanding of its importance, we can see what such deliberations might look like. What follows is a non-exhaustive list of when machine explainability does and doesn't matter. As you'll see, these are not strict rules, but rules of thumb.

When Machine Explainability *Doesn't* Matter

When your model doesn't directly deal with decisions about how anyone should be treated

Let's take a case in which you're using ML to predict the delivery dates of shipments of screws for your toy manufacturing facility. In that case, there's probably not a ton of ethical risk at stake. Your predictions are about delivery times, not about people, and while its predictions may indirectly cause you to treat some people poorly (depending on who you blame when there's a delay), there's nothing inherently ethically risky about making predictions about your supply chain. What you really care about is accuracy, so you may reasonably decide that machine explainability doesn't need to be prioritized. To the extent that you do think it's important, it may be for nonethical reasons; for example, explainable models are easier to debug.

When people explanations for why you want to use a black box plus informed consent justifies use

Making stock market predictions is ethically risky because those predictions can lead investors and financial advisers to recommend investments that wind up bankrupting people. Still, you might think as follows: "Accuracy is of the utmost importance, and if we made our model explainable, we'd have to decrease accuracy so much that it wouldn't be worth it anymore. Further, we can be transparent with our advisees about all the people explanations and that we have no machine explanations, and then they can determine whether they're willing to take the risk. If they give us their informed consent to use the black box, then we've treated them respectfully and the results are on them, for better or worse."

Also, consider a cancer-diagnosing ML that's 99.9 percent accurate. It plays a crucial role in doctors saving tens or even hundreds of thousands of lives every year compared to the best explainable model (or non-ML cancer-diagnosing techniques). Are we ethically required to provide machine explanations in addition to the people explanations? Would you prefer the incredibly accurate black box ML or the less accurate glass box ML for determining whether you have cancer? Plausibly, if doctors provide the people explanations and secure your informed consent on using the black box, it's ethically permissible to use it.

One lesson to take from this is that it can be reasonable to trust a black box model on the condition that it performs well against robust and relevant benchmarks. You may even find some black box models more trustworthy than humans in certain contexts. We have to be very careful, however. While there are some cases in which people explanations conjoined with informed consent justify deploying the black box, there are plausibly some cases in which that is *not* sufficient. For instance, even if your black box ML is very accurate at predicting the likelihood of recidivism, the state may nonetheless have a justified interest in barring use of that black box, even if individual citizens give their informed consent to be judged by it instead of by a human. That's because the state has an interest in securing procedural justice—ensuring that the processes by which people are found guilty or innocent, granted or denied bail, and so on are fair procedures—and the inability to know how inputs are transformed to outputs may be objectionable precisely because they are not capable of being judged as procedurally (un)fair.

When Machine Explainability *Does* Matter

When expressing respect is ethically required

In health care, respect for persons is required and manifests itself in practice, in part, by ensuring that people's informed consent is secured before a procedure is performed. In other cases, expressing respect for people is a great thing to do but not ethically required. Walking up to a speaker after their talk and telling them you respect them and their work is an expression of respect, but it's certainly not ethically required; no one will blame you for not doing it, as they would if you remove their spleen without their informed consent.

There are surely cases in which respect requires us to provide explanations for machine outputs. When the Machine spit out a "Nope" after "reviewing" your mortgage application, you would be justified in feeling insulted. The same goes if you're denied parole or a raise. There are certain decisions for which we think that, particularly in those cases in which we've been harmed in some way, we're *owed* an explanation. One central question to ask is thus, "Will the ML outputs, or what people will decide in light of those outputs, potentially wrong people or deprive them of an important opportunity or benefit (e.g., a job interview)?" If the answer is yes, that's a pretty good indication you need to provide an explanation.

When people need to know how to get better results

Machine explanations are important not only to express respect, but also because they can be utilized in various ways. Again, if the outputs or the decisions made can wrong people or deprive them of an opportunity, then it may be important to explain why they received the verdict they did so they can attempt to make changes that result in a different verdict the next time, for example, prioritizing paying off their loans over overdue parking fines because it turns out the former, and not the latter, are relevant to getting denied the loan.

When people need to know how to approach and make a decision

Suppose your fraud department uses AI to detect fraud, and it brings those red-flag cases to people who will make the final judgment about whether to pull the alarm. Those people will likely have to know why the AI is flagging it to know what they should pay attention to so they can perform their job efficiently.

When the outputs are strange

The predictions the ML makes are, to mere mortals, utterly . . . unpredictable.

For instance, suppose that insanely accurate cancer-diagnosing ML offers predictions that don't cohere with the predictions of our best oncologists. The ML has determined that you have a 93 percent chance of having cancer, but your world-renowned doctors just don't see the evidence. We have the people explanations, we lack the machine explanation, we know how well the ML tests, but this prediction is just so odd.

There are two options: eschew the ML predictions in favor of human expertise or defer to the ML. On the one hand, experts are experts for a reason: they have a wealth of knowledge, experience, and skill and so have earned our trust, especially when there is consensus among the experts. What's more, sometimes ML recognizes correlations among variables that are utterly coincidental and so not, in fact, predictive. The ML then mistakenly uses those variables in predicting new cases. Then again, experts are not all-knowing, and there's always the possibility that the model is recognizing a predictive pattern that humans simply have not picked up on or even cannot pick up on.[2] Perhaps if we can explain *why* the ML is predicting that you have cancer, we could better evaluate it.

Unfortunately, even that's not so simple. Imagine that cancer-diagnosing ML noticed a correlation between decreasing frequency of social media posting and cancer. That's odd, but we can tell some kind of story to explain it. Cancer has an overall deleterious impact on one's system, which impacts one's energy levels, which impacts the frequency with which you post. So is "decreased social media posting" a predictive variable that the machines picked up on but we never would? Or is that just total nonsense and we should regard this ML as defective?

Data scientists often reply by insisting that we need ML that picks up on causal patterns, not simply correlations among variables. But that reply is something of a nonstarter. The reason is that causal relationships can be phenomenally complex, so complex, in fact, that the number of links in a chain are too great for we mere mortals to grasp. The story I told about cancer and energy levels is, after all, a causal story. But is this causal story true? The fact that it's a causal story instead of a correlation story doesn't help us in determining the answer to that question.

What people will do with the outputs plays a role in whether you need to give an explanation and how to articulate that explanation. That said, the explanations may not always be as enlightening as you'd like; you may not know how to react to the pattern the ML alleges is predictive. In such cases, we may have to prioritize people explanations and informed consent with regard to risk-taking in using the machine outputs in human decision-making.

When you need to justify treatment

Let's return to Marvin denying you a loan. Sometimes the explanations show that a person or a team or an organization as a whole was justified in making the decision they did: "There was a huge influx of applications, we couldn't afford to hire more people, and we didn't have the time to onboard those we could, our business model and considerations of fairness require that we don't turn people away at the door" and so on. At other times, the explanations show that they were not justified. If the executive who decided to deploy the AI said, "Well, I wasn't sure if I should approve the model for deployment because this technical stuff is really beyond me, but I thought, 'To hell with it, these guys are smart; let's rock and roll,'" then we probably think the executive was unjustified in deciding as he did. In fact, he was downright reckless.

Explanations are deeply important when we want to assess whether a certain kind of treatment is justified, be it from an ethical, regulatory, or legal perspective. When it comes to machine explanations, we now need to ask two questions that pertain to the two kinds of machine explanations.

1. With regards to global explanations: Are the ML rules—what turns inputs into outputs—justifiable?
   - Suppose the ML learns, with the help of social media data, that historically, those people who have defaulted on loans correlates with those people who have parents that have defaulted on loans, and so uses "has parents that have defaulted on loans" as part of its calculations for determining the probability that you will default on yours. Should the fact that your parents defaulted on their loans bear on whether you should get a loan? There is that high correlation, let's suppose, but that seems deeply unfair. In fact, it looks like a great way to ensure and reinforce intergenerational poverty and, relatedly, structural racism.
2. With regards to local explanations: Was this particular output about this particular person justified?
   - Let's assume for one moment, solely for the sake of argument, that using your parent's loan history is justifiable in determining whether you get a loan. As it turns out, the social media data was misleading: due to multiple records of people with your last name, it thought these loan-defaulting parents are yours when in fact those loan-*paying* parents are yours. As a result, you were judged unfairly because of inaccurate data.

Questions pertaining to whether the global and local explanations are also *justifications* are difficult to answer. And crucially, while there are technical tools that help to explain how this particular variable played a role in the output, there are no technical tools to assess the justifiability of the rules. The question whether some set of rules is justified is not a question for data scientists. It's a question for ethicists, regulators, lawyers, and ultimately, anyone at all who is concerned about whether the game they're being asked or even required to play is governed by rules they can accept. This brings us to another Structure from Content Lesson.

> **Structure from Content Lesson #6:** In cases in which it's important to have global explanations—those that articulate the rules of the game for how inputs are turned into outputs—you should have those with ethical and legal expertise involved in an assessment of the fairness of the rules.

What Makes Explanations Good Explanations?

You've determined that, for some particular use case, a machine explanation is needed. Your job isn't done yet, though. For all of those cases in which machine explanations matter, you'll have to decide what kind of explanation is needed to be useful and how to communicate that explanation. Put differently, what constitutes a *good* (machine) explanation?

Good explanations are those that speak to one or more of the features that make explanations important in the first place. A good explanation will sufficiently demonstrate respect, allow the user of the AI or the people impacted by the AI to make well-informed decisions, and allow people to assess whether the rules that govern the decision are fair, good, reasonable, or just. You will also need to consider the following three criteria for a good explanation: truth, ease of use, and intelligibility.

Truth

One obvious criterion is that the explanation has to be true or, at least, true *enough*. Some technical tools offer explanations for what's going on inside the black box, but they are only *approximations* of what's going on. In some cases, that's fine; for example, if we're using those tools so that we can debug the model and those approximations give us enough of what we need to successfully debug. In other cases, especially high-risk cases (for example, in the criminal justice system), you need more than an approximation.

Other questions loom large. How many true statements do you need to offer? What true statements can you justifiably exclude? How accurate does the explanation need to be? Answering these questions requires a qualitative assessment. Whether something is justifiably omitted from the explanation depends on whether that information is a nice-to-have or need-to-have for expressing respect and enabling the end user to make better decisions or assess whether the rules are fair.

Ease, efficiency, and effectiveness of use

Take the example of the employee who is reviewing the case flagged by the ML as a potential instance of fraud. That person needs an explanation so they can determine whether this flag is a true or false positive; they need to know where they should start looking. Since the explanation needs to be *useful*, you'll need to think about how "deep" the explanation should go. Too deep and you're not only decreasing accuracy too much but also confusing the recipient of that explanation who doesn't have time to read a twenty-page document on each case of potential fraud detection. Too shallow and the explanation only decreases accuracy a bit and doesn't help the user. What counts as a usable and, hence, good explanation then? You need to work with those end users to understand what and how much information they need; what counts as a good explanation for them is determined by their task.

I saw this up close when I worked with a client that was developing AI software to help HR managers monitor employee emails for inappropriate content. Ethical risks abound, insofar as there are concerns around privacy violations, surveillance, and bias, but there was also an issue regarding the explainability of their AI's output. I was hired to identify the ethical risks of the product and worked with the engineers, data scientists, and product developers to make changes in the product and recommendations on how to (not) deploy it.

The AI was, at its core, a sentiment-analysis tool. It "read" emails and scored the dozens of emotions or attitudes it manifested, including respect, generosity, friendliness, aggressiveness, and so on.

With regard to explainability, there were two issues. What kinds of explanations do the executives who approve purchasing this software need? In general, they need to know that the rules of the game are fair and accurate. They need global explanations. The HR managers who would actually use the software, on the other hand, need local explanations. They need to know why, exactly, *this* email was flagged.

Actually, that's partly true. The executives need explanations of the rules of the game to ensure fairness and efficacy. The HR managers may not need to know why it was flagged. After all, it's their responsibility to read the flagged email, understand its context, and make a judgment as to the appropriate course of action.

My recommendation (with regard to explainability at least; there were other issues we dealt with regarding privacy and bias) was twofold:

1. Interview the target users of the software, that is, HR managers, to determine what, if any, kinds of explanations they need and why.
2. Ensure that in the onboarding process those HR managers are informed of the ethical best practices for use of the software, which includes a responsibility to understand the context in which that email was sent and not to simply reward or discipline staff based on the AI's outputs.

Intelligibility

Once you know what kind of explanation you need to give—whether it concerns the rules of the game or why this particular set of inputs led to this particular output—and how important it is that the person receive that explanation, you'll also need to think about how to articulate the explanation. If I owe you an explanation for why I mistreated you, and I give you that explanation in ancient Greek (which, let's wildly suppose, you can't understand), then while I've given an explanation, there's a relevant sense in which I haven't given it *to you*. After all, the goal of explaining something to someone is, standardly, to get them to understand the thing you're explaining. This means that the kind of machine explanation you offer has to be tailored to the intended audience. Data scientists speak the language of mathematical formulas that laypeople and regulators usually don't understand, and the existing explainability tools they use threaten to render the explanations they generate as irrelevant to explainees. Once again, one of the criteria for a good explanation varies by context: what your audience is capable of understanding.

The need to give true explanations that are easy to use and readily intelligible to your audience shows us another Structure from Content Lesson.

> **Structure from Content Lesson #7:** Consult the end users of the AI software you're developing to determine whether an explanation is needed and, if so, what a good explanation looks like given their knowledge base, skills, and purposes.

Where'd All Those Inputs Come from, Anyway?

We've talked about discriminatory outputs. We've talked about the opacity of what happens before those outputs. Now it's time to talk about those potentially ill-gotten inputs and, more generally, how we can avoid violating people's privacy in training AI and choosing what kind of AIs to make in the first place.

Recap

- The three Structure from Content Lessons that relate to explainability and can guide approaches to Structure that are gleaned from understanding Content:

1. You need the right people to determine whether people explanations, global machine explanations, local machine explanations, or all of the above are important for a given use case.

2. In cases in which it's important to have global explanations—those that articulate the rules of the game for how inputs are turned into outputs—you should have those with ethical and legal expertise involved in an assessment of the fairness of the rules.

3. Consult the end users of the AI software you're developing to determine whether an explanation is needed and, if so, what a good explanation looks like given their knowledge base, skills, and purposes.

- Explanations for ML outputs and how those outputs affect people through what people do with those outputs involve two kinds of explanations:
  - People explanations are about the decisions people make in developing and deploying the model, why they do what they do with the outputs, and so on.
  - Machine explanations are about what goes on between the inputs and the outputs. One kind of machine explanation, global explanations, concerns the rules that govern the system; how it treats inputs in such a way that it leads to outputs. Another kind of machine explanation, local explanations, concerns how some particular set of inputs leads to a particular output.

- Machine explainability often comes at a cost, for example, reduced accuracy and an increase in resources devoted to making the ML model explainable.
- Explanations, including machine explanations, are ethically important for at least three reasons (in those cases where it is important):
  - They express respect for the person to whom you're explaining.
  - They enable the explainee to change their behavior or make various decisions so they can have some control over what kind of decision they'll receive in the future.
  - They enable people to assess whether the rules of the model that govern how inputs are turned into outputs are justifiable from ethical, reputational, regulatory, and legal perspectives.
- Organizations need to determine, for each particular use case, whether explainability is important and, if so, how important it is in relation to other goals, for example, accuracy. Rules of thumb include:
  - Machine explainability is not needed when:
    - Your model doesn't directly deal with decisions about how anyone should be treated.
    - People explanations for why you want to use a black box plus informed consent makes use ethically permissible.
  - Machine explainability is needed when:
    - Expressing respect is ethically required.
    - People need to know how to get better results.

- *People need to know how to approach and make a decision.*
- *The outputs are very strange.*
- *You need to justify treatment (from an ethical, regulatory, or legal perspective).*

- The criteria for good explanations include being:
  - True (or true enough for the case at hand)
  - Easy, efficient, and effective for its intended use
  - Intelligible to the intended audience
- Talking about explanations immediately gives rise to questions about the justification of decisions, actions, processes, and so on. Organizations need to determine who the right people are to make those assessments, keeping in mind that data scientists and engineers are simply not the experts on such topics.

4

Privacy

Ascending the Five Ethical Levels

Imagine you move into a Covid-friendly office building. It's circular, and the offices are along the edge of the circle. The inside-facing wall of your office is glass and faces an opaque structure at the middle of the circle, one that runs from the ground floor to the very top of the building. Inside that structure there is at least one supervisor, observing people's behavior through their glass wall. Given the design of the building, you can't see who is watching you or even whether someone is watching you, though they can see you.

The supervisor(s) have three responsibilities and one broad goal.

Responsibility one is to learn various things about you by observation. When you have your lunch, what you eat, who you interact with, and so on.

Responsibility two is to extrapolate from that information certain other facts about you, for example, whether you might quit soon, how likely you are to become pregnant in the next year, whether you might be interested in the new cafeteria offerings, and so on.

And responsibility three is to use that information to create new tools that will allow them to collect even more information about you that will in turn fuel new predictions and inventions, and so on, ad infinitum.

Finally, their broad goal is to use all of this information and these tools so they can make various decisions and recommendations related to you: whether you get a raise, promotion, or bonus, what they offer you at the cafeteria, how many reminder emails they'll send you about trying the new office gym, whether you were overly aggressive in a conversation with colleagues, whether you might need the services of a mental health expert, and so on.

You're probably not particularly comfortable with any of this. You probably think it's a violation of your privacy, that the supervisors don't have your best interests at heart (perhaps all their recommendations center around what they think will make you more productive so they can extract the maximum value from you, independently of what that does to your health or well-being), and that all of this impinges on your autonomy—your ability to live your life freely, without the undue influence of others.

As you have already discerned, these kinds of concerns are exactly the ones raised in the context of talking about privacy and machine learning.

At the core of ML is data, and the more of it, the better for those training their models. This means that companies that want to profit from you are *highly* incentivized to collect as much data as possible about you and the way you behave. In fact, companies will collect people's data without even knowing exactly what they'll use it for, or even if they ever will. They collect it *just in case* they can wring some value from it down the line. The value doesn't even have to come directly from how they use it; it can come from selling the data to someone else who thinks they have a use for it.

The fact that you don't know what data is collected about you and who has access to it is already troublesome. In some cases, it will constitute a violation of privacy, as when your location, financial, or medical history is revealed to parties you never wanted to see those details (your ex-spouse, for instance).

All of that data is then used to train ML models that make predictions about you that in turn influences how those organizations treat you. Perhaps your social media data is used to train models that determine whether you get a mortgage. They determine what news articles bubble up to the top of your search inquiries, what YouTube video is recommended next, what job, housing, and restaurant ads you see, and so on. Insofar as your life consists in choosing options from a menu, and most of that menu is found online, you'll be choosing among options *they*—the aggregate of all those companies collecting and selling all your data while also using it to train their AI to make increasingly accurate predictions about what will get you to click, share, and buy—have chosen for you.

Sometimes using ML and other tools to predict how to get you to stay on a site and click is referred to as the "attention economy." The more they can control how much attention they get from you, the better they do. And sometimes the data gathering involved in developing AI is referred to as the "surveillance economy." The more they know about you, the better they can influence you. In truth, both economies are part of the same market. Companies surveil, in part, so they can figure out how to get your attention, so they can direct you to do things that will drive their bottom line.

Finally, all that data and ML is used to create particular products that threaten to invade people's privacy. The one on the top of most everyone's list is facial-recognition software, which can potentially pick your face out of a crowd and identify you. Notoriously, the startup Clearview AI collected over 3 billion images of people from Facebook, YouTube, Venmo, and millions of other websites. Those with access to its software can take a picture of someone in public, upload it to the app, and it will return all of the publicly available photos of that person online along with links to where those photos can be found, including sites that might also include your name, address, and other personal information.

These kinds of privacy issues have received a tremendous amount of attention in recent years. Citizens, consumers, employees, and governments are taking note. Newspaper articles and social media posts abound detailing the various ways corporations trample privacy interests and rights. Various regulations have been passed to protect people's data—most notably, the General Data Protection Regulation (GDPR) in the EU and the California Consumer Privacy Act (CCPA)—and other regulations are in the pipeline, such as recent recommendations to EU member states on AI or ML regulations.

Some companies have handled the issue . . . poorly. Facebook's reputation suffered not only from the Cambridge Analytica saga—which would be an existential threat for most any company other than a financial behemoth like Facebook—but from subsequent events that continually tarnish its reputation. Other companies have fared better. Apple, for instance, has turned its stance on privacy into a major element of its brand.

In my experience, most companies handle the issue poorly by virtue of *misunderstanding* what privacy is all about.

Disambiguating "Privacy"

One of the problems with talking about "privacy" with engineers, data scientists, and senior leaders is that they don't hear the word in the way most citizens hear it. That's because the term is multiply ambiguous, or put slightly differently, privacy has three sides.

One way to think about privacy is in terms of compliance with regulations and the law, for example, compliance with GDPR and CCPA. By complying, someone with this mindset thinks, you have achieved respecting people's privacy. A second way is to think about it in terms of cybersecurity: what practices one has for keeping data safe from those who should not have access to it (e.g., various employees, hackers, governments, etc.). By preventing unwanted and unwarranted access, someone with this mindset thinks, you have sufficiently respected people's privacy. And the third way to think about privacy is from an ethical risk perspective.

While there are overlapping areas in the Venn diagram of these three aspects of privacy, they are clearly distinct. For our purposes, it's important to explore this third version and see what ethical risks arise that are distinct from compliance and cybersecurity.

First, ethical risks remain even with regulations like GDPR and CCPA, because those only have effect in certain jurisdictions: EU member states and California, respectively. Even if it were the case that the set of ethical risks is identical to the set of regulatory violation risks of either of these, there remains the simple fact that much of the United States is unaffected by them. This means that a company can operate in ways incompatible with CCPA in all states except California, and thus those ethical risks remain a threat.

Second, even beyond jurisdiction, it's not the case that ethical risks with regard to privacy are identical to the regulatory risks. For instance, various bans on facial-recognition software are recommended by the EU precisely because those recommendations are not contained in GDPR. Nonetheless, various companies have been criticized in the news and social media for their use of that technology.

Third, ethical risks remain because unwarranted access risks aren't the only cybersecurity risks relating to data and AI. Again, facial-recognition software potentially constitutes a threat to privacy independently of concerns about sloppy data controls or the threat of a data leak or hack. Perhaps more worrying than facial-recognition software is lip-reading AI, which can discern what people are saying without being within ear- or, one might say, microphone-shot.[1] And things get even worse if the way people move their mouths, jaws, tongues, and so on acts as a kind of fingerprint, in which case a camera enhanced with this software can identify who is saying what. These are privacy risks that are neither regulated against nor relevant to cyber risks.

None of this implies that compliance and security are not important. Defying regulations is expensive. It costs resources to accommodate investigations and pay fines, and headlines announcing those investigations and fines tarnishes brands. Cybersecurity has similar consequences. A system in which user, patient, consumer, or citizen data is leaked or hacked is an expensive problem. And both are ethically problematic. Neither set of risks, however, is identical to the set of ethical risks we reference when we talk about privacy in the context of data and AI ethics.

Privacy Is Not Just about Anonymity

In some cases, engineers, data scientists, and other technologists will talk about anonymity as the key to respecting privacy, including in the context of a discussion on AI ethics, which in turn invites technical conversations about how to anonymize the data with the smallest probability of being de-anonymized.

We've seen this before. In talking about bias, technologists think a mathematical tool will identify and mitigate bias. It isn't true. In talking about explainability, technologists think a mathematical tool will turn the black box transparent. It isn't true. So, when technologists reduce the ethical risk of privacy to an issue of anonymity and then search for mathematical tools to anonymize data—for example, differential privacy, k-anonymity, I-diversity, and cryptographic hashings—we should be suspicious.

The main assumption technologists make is that, *If I don't know whose data this is, then I can't be violating anyone's privacy.*

The assumption is not entirely unreasonable. When an organization or individual knows you by name, or any other personally identifiable information (PII), that makes it easier to track you across websites (for instance) and to build a profile of you with increasing quantities of information. That said, in the context of data and AI ethics, the assumption is false. We can see how by thinking about Facebook's Cambridge Analytica scandal.

Cambridge Analytica collected the data of over 87 million Facebook users, 70.6 million of whom were in the United States. Cambridge Analytica used that data to create psychological profiles, which were in turn used to predict what kind of political ad would influence which kinds of people in a given location, for example, what kinds of ads would incline them to vote for Donald Trump. That Facebook designed its product in a way that would allow Cambridge Analytica to collect that information with the app it uploaded to the platform was widely seen as a privacy violation; Facebook should not have shared that information with Cambridge Analytica. Note that Facebook wasn't hacked in the cybersecurity sense of that term. It simply didn't take privacy into account or, at least, not in the right way or to the right extent, when designing its systems.

Is this massive breach of privacy about anonymity? I don't see how. Cambridge Analytica doesn't need to have anyone in the organization know the names of any of the users. In fact, it could have, for the sake of maintaining profile anonymity, intentionally encrypted or hashed the username and other PII. To Cambridge Analytica, all it has is "User fe79n583025nk will, with a probability of 74.3 percent, find ad #23 persuasive." If that were the case, would Facebook users, citizens, and government officials find no issue with Cambridge Analytica, which mined the data, or Facebook, which designed its software in such a way that Cambridge Analytica had the level of access it did? Somehow, I doubt it.

The moral of the story is not that anonymity doesn't matter. It's that it can't be all that matters. That's because anonymity is not sufficient to stop companies, governments, and other organizations from collecting data about you, training its ML with your data, making predictions about you, and making various decisions on how to treat you. More specifically, what's at issue is the increasing degree of power or *control* companies have by virtue of the data they collect and the AI they create: control over who gets an interview or housing, what content people consume, what ads they see, who people vote for, what those people believe about the legitimacy of elections, and so on.

If you knew what data companies are collecting and what they're doing with it, and you had the control to stop them from either collecting it in the first place or using it in ways to which you object, you could, at least in part, protect yourself from undue manipulation and being treated in a way to which you object. Further, if you knew how *economically valuable* your data was to those organizations, you might require compensation for the collection and use of your data. If your data is an asset, you probably don't want to give it away for free (just as you'd be opposed to this with regard to any other asset). At the end of the day, privacy talk in AI ethics is not about what companies know about citizens. It's about control. More specifically, it's about the right to control who can collect what data about you and what they can use it for.

Privacy Is a Capacity

When you pull down your shades in your bedroom, you are *exercising* your right to privacy, and you are similarly exercising that right when you retract the shades. Relatedly, when you invite someone into your bedroom (presumably with the shades down), that person is not violating your privacy. That's because privacy is a right (or perhaps an interest) that you can act on.

This conception of privacy is codified in the law, which articulates a distinction between informational privacy and constitutional privacy.

Informational privacy concerns a right to control information about yourself: who has it, for how long, and under what conditions. Such control is deemed important so that people can protect themselves from, for instance, unwarranted searches and surveillance. Constitutional privacy is not about control over information about oneself but rather about control over *oneself*. Insofar as we have such a right, it is a right to exhibit a certain level of independence in how our lives unfold, with whom we associate, what kind of lifestyle we prefer. Such a right has been used to defend, for instance, being gay, whether to have children and, if so, how many, and whether to practice a religion.

If your company has respecting privacy as one of its goals, then that means, *at a bare minimum*, not deploying AI in such a way that this capacity to control (information about) oneself is either undermined or cannot be exercised without great effort on the part of the user, consumer, or citizen. At a *maximum*, it means deploying AI that positively promotes or enables the exercise of that capacity.

Let's suppose you work for an organization that claims to respect people and their privacy. You don't want to undermine people's capacity to exercise their right to privacy. You might want to maximally empower their capacity to exercise that right. Or you may want something in between. How do we measure such things, though, and how do we infuse it into the development and deployment of AI?

The Five Ethical Levels of Privacy

We start by thinking about the elements that create the conditions under which your users, consumers, or citizens can exercise their capacity to control their (digital) lives.

Transparency

If users, consumers, or citizens don't know what information is being collected about them, what's being done with it, what decisions they contribute to, who it's being shared with or sold to, then they cannot possibly exercise any control. If, as a business, you haven't told customers or, worse, you don't know either, that's a problem.

Data control

Users, consumers, or citizens may or may not have the ability to correct, edit, or delete information about themselves and may or may not be able to opt out of being treated in a certain way (e.g., opting out of targeted ads). Having the capacity to perform these actions is at least *part* of what is involved in exercising control over one's information. Giving the capacity is increasingly important for companies, for at least three reasons. First, that ability is required by some regulations, for example, GDPR. Second, it communicates to users (or consumers or citizens, hereafter I'll say "users" to represent all three) that you respect their privacy. And third, it gives users an opportunity to fix inaccurate information you have about them, which will enable you to serve them better and create more accurate AI models.

Opt in or out by default

Most companies collect a great deal of data by default. It might happen during a registration process. It may happen as a user is active on your site, where your organization collects data about where they go on the site, for how long, what they click on, and so on. This happens without any choice by the user; they are automatically "opted in" for such data collection. The alternative is for companies to automatically "opt out" their users from data collection and requiring users to opt in to such data collection. The former approach puts the burden on the user to investigate how to obtain the data the organization has about them, to review that list, and to opt out of the organization's collection of some set of data or using it for some set of purposes. The latter approach puts the burden on your organization to demonstrate to the user that they will sufficiently benefit from sharing that data and using it in the proposed ways such that it is a good decision for them to opt in to sharing their data. Opting out by default is motivated, in part, by the thought that, first, do no harm, and you can do that by not assuming you have the user's consent to collect and use their data.

Full services

Your organization may increase or decrease the services it provides depending on what data a person provides. Some organizations will not provide any services if you do not consent to their privacy (intrusive) policies. Some will vary the degree of services provided depending on how much data the user shares. Some will provide full services independently of how much data the user shares. One concern here has to do with how essential the services are. If autonomy consists in, at least in part, your ability to live your life freely, without the undue influence of others, and an organization provides an essential service on the condition that you provide them with a level of access to your data that you're not comfortable with, then the organization is exhibiting an undue influence on you; your autonomy is being impinged upon.

With these elements of privacy articulated, we can see what I call The Five Ethical Levels of Privacy, captured in table 4-1.

Level One: Blindfolded and handcuffed consumer. People are *in the dark* and *passive* with regard to their data and the predictions made

TABLE 4-1

The five ethical levels of privacy

	Level 1 *Blindfolded and handcuffed*	Level 2 *Handcuffed*	Level 3 *Pressured*	Level 4 *Slightly curtailed*	Level 5 *Grateful*
Transparency		✔	✔	✔	✔
Data control			✔	✔	✔
Opt out by default				✔	✔
Full services	✔	✔			✔

about them. This is the standard state of affairs. The vast majority of consumers scarcely know what data is, let alone what "metadata" or "artificial intelligence" or "machine learning" or "predictive algorithms" are. And even if they were educated on such matters, the average person is not familiar with the privacy policies of the dozens if not hundreds of sites and apps they interact with regularly. What's more, data can be collected about people and predictions made about them despite their not choosing to be on a website or purchase anything. Corporate surveillance of employees (as caricatured at the start of this chapter) is performed in a way that is not transparent, so employees lack control and they are opted in by default. Citizens surveilled by a police force—which we'll discuss in more detail in chapter 7—are in the same boat.

For those users or consumers whose data is collected because of their use of a website or app, it is no argument for the claim that level one has been surpassed because there are "terms and conditions" and privacy policies that people "accept" when they click on a banner asking for their acceptance. While this may or may not protect companies legally, it does not protect them from ethical or reputational risk. Had Facebook's terms and conditions indicated the possibility of a Cambridge Analytica–type incident, it would have done little to ebb the flood of criticism that came its way. Indeed, had it announced, "Well, we told you it was possible in our thirty-page terms and conditions written in legalese," that would have only drawn more ire. As we saw in the previous chapter, in order to be effective and convey respect, explanations need to be intelligible and digestible to their audiences.

When companies operate at level one, they are engaging in the kind of activity that tends to enrage people on social media and excite journalists. It inspires books like *Surveillance Capitalism* and the *New York Times*'s "Privacy Project," in which articles are continuously written on the ways in which corporations breach citizen and consumer trust. It's what allows Apple to ridicule Facebook.

Level two: Handcuffed consumer. At least the blindfold is off. People are, in principle, *knowledgeable* about their data and predictions made about them, but they are still *passive* with regards to what is collected and what is done with their data. Information about their data and relevant predictions are accessible to them, should they put in a little effort. The company collecting their data has gone to some trouble in articulating for the user what data it has about them and what it's using it for. That said, at this level, while people know what's being done with their data, they can't do anything about it. This is roughly the condition you're in with the Department of Motor Vehicles. It has a lot of data about you—name, home address, height, hair and eye color, number of times you've been charged with the misdemeanor of reckless driving. You can't do much about this, though.

Level three: Pressured consumer. People know what's being done *and* they have some degree of control over what data is collected and how it's used. More specifically, after their investigation of such matters, they have the capacity to opt out of the organization collecting data and using it in ways to which they object. That said, since they need to opt out, this means some set of data has already been collected and put to various uses before the person engages in their investigation and opts out.

Level four: Slightly curtailed consumer. People have knowledge, and their data isn't collected or used without their consent being obtained.

Notice that, in levels one and two—where people have no control over what data is collected or what's done with it, except to not use the services or goods of the company at all—full services are provided. And this is where most companies are. The rationale is "so long as we're providing value to the customer, we're justified in using their data when they use our services." The *judgment*, in this case, as to whether the services provided are worth the sharing of data, is made by the company itself, which has a financial incentive to make that judgment.

At levels three and four—where people can opt in or out—the judgment is, more or less, made by the consumers whose data is being collected. They gain control. But companies can incentivize (or pressure, depending on the urgency with which people need to use the service) people to make that trade by curtailing services in response to curtailed sharing of data. This is a little like seducing someone you know is married; yes, it's their decision, but you've actively played a role in getting them to make a decision that results in breaking a promise to their spouse.

Level five: Free and grateful consumer. The organization provides full services independently of what data the person opts in to provide and consents to be used for various purposes (except for data required to deliver the services for which the person has requested or paid for). This is compatible, of course, with curtailing services because the person has not provided payment for those services.

These five levels are a heuristic. Reality is much more complex. In some cases, organizations are (rightfully) committed to different levels for different products. And they may be transparent in this respect but not in another one (e.g., transparent about what data is collected but opaque about what predictions they're making). Still, they give us a grip on what privacy in AI ethics is really about. What's more, the different levels highlight the need for organizations to determine what level the organization strives for (or, more importantly, what level they never want to fall below), both at the organizational level and on a per-product basis. This brings us to a Structure from Content Lesson.

> **Structure from Content Lesson #8:** Before you start collecting data to train your AI, determine what ethical level of ethical privacy is appropriate for the use case.

Building and Deploying with Five Ethical Levels of Privacy

The Five Ethical Levels of Privacy provide a way of assessing the degree of privacy respected by the product and, indirectly, the organization that created the product, which is good both for external stakeholders and for executives and managers charged with ensuring the organizational commitment to privacy is made real. It is also a tool by which developers can think about privacy as it is developed.

Suppose your product managers have a clear understanding of what your organization's commitment to privacy looks like, including what kinds of things it will always do and what kinds of things it will never do (an understanding it may arrive at from your AI Ethics Statement, which we'll discuss in detail in the next chapter). It may even include a commitment to never falling below level two of privacy, or a rabid commitment to level five.

A problem is presented to one of your AI teams, and they get to work brainstorming or—to use a "word" that, when used, should result in the loss of one's tongue—*ideating* potential solutions. As they think about those solutions, they also think about what levels of privacy those proposed solutions are compatible with and how the proposed product fits into your organization's general privacy commitments. Some proposed solutions—like the one that secretly deploys facial-recognition technology so as to identify shoppers in the store so it can send discount codes for toilet paper, good for one hour, to their phones—are rejected because the organization requires transparency with its customers. Other solutions—like the one that texts discount codes for toilet paper to preexisting customers based on when the AI predicts they probably need more—are left on the table because those customers have already opted in to having that data collected for the purposes of receiving targeted discount codes, which reflects the organization's commitment to level four (since customers are opted out by default but they also won't get discount codes without opting in).

In some cases, what level a company operates at is largely determined by its business model. In the case of Facebook, it might crumble if it stopped collecting user data unless people opted in while providing full services to everyone. Its revenue is driven through serving ads, and advertisers need user data so they can target them. Other businesses, for example, those that operate on a subscription model, can afford to reach level five.

Not all companies should strive for level five. Privacy, conceived of as the extent to which the people you collect data about and on whom you deploy your AI have knowledge and control over what data your organization collects and what it does with it, is something worth valuing. But it is not the only thing worth valuing, and there are cases in which it is reasonable to decrease the level of privacy you reach for the sake of some other (ethical) good that outweighs it. If, for instance, decreasing the level of privacy you reach is essential to, say, developing a vaccine for a global pandemic, then your choice may well be ethically justified (on the condition that, for instance, you've been responsible with the security of the data and the AI infrastructure you've built). In fact, Facebook is arguably justified—*to some extent*—in its privacy practices, given that its business model, which is advertising based, not subscription based, makes it economically feasible to provide its services globally. Citizens of developing countries with extremely low or no wages can use Facebook for personal and work-related reasons without having to shoulder an additional financial burden. Were Facebook to introduce a global subscription model in the name of privacy, it would no doubt come under the criticism, which would not be unreasonable, that it has now excluded the historically and currently marginalized citizens of the global community.

In this respect, Facebook is in a bit of a bind. One of the things it's forced to do is to weigh two values that are in conflict (and putting the financial calculations to the side): privacy, on the one hand, which can be increased with a subscription model, and providing opportunities to those desperately in need of opportunity, on the other hand, which counsels against a subscription model. How to resolve this tension is not easy, and it's certainly not in the job description of data scientists and engineers to resolve it. We thus have another Structure from Content Lesson.

> **Structure from Content Lesson #9:** Your organization needs an individual or, ideally, a set of individuals, that can make responsible, expert-informed decisions when ethical values conflict.

Creepy Companies and Respect

We've spent this chapter focusing on an essential element for thinking about privacy from an ethical perspective: who controls the data and what it's used for. But for a lot of people, their concerns about their privacy being violated aren't formulated in quite this way. Instead, people characterize all the data that your organization and others collect about them as being . . . *creepy*. It's "icky" that companies are "stalking" their consumers. And consumers may reject companies for collecting their data for just that reason.

Myself, I'm inclined to think these concerns are somewhat misguided. Being creepy is to *appear* dangerous or unsafe or threatening. There's then the further question whether the creepy thing really *is* a threat. (Some people are creepy but harmless; they make eye contact for too long, for instance, but there's nothing nefarious behind the stare.) And as I've said, the real danger is how organizations use that data, not merely in the fact that they have it. You might think, then, "Well, our organization isn't doing anything ethically problematic with their data so their concerns about us being creepy or threatening are ill-founded; thus, we can, ethically speaking, ignore their complaints about creepiness." But in that, you'd be wrong.

Your consumers may or may not have unfounded concerns about what you'll do with their data. They find it creepy, and you think their feelings of creepiness are unwarranted. But *respecting* people entails, in part, that you respect their wishes, even if you think their wishes are misguided or ill-informed. To simply wave away their concerns is to substitute your organization's judgment for theirs, and even if that judgment is more accurate, failing to respect their wishes can be objectionably paternalistic.

A Final Thought: The Oddness of Talking about Privacy

I have to admit that—putting regulatory compliance and cybersecurity to the side—I find talk about privacy in the context of AI a bit odd. The real danger for users, consumers, and citizens is not so much that organizations *have* certain data about them, but rather that organizations—including yours—may *do* things with that data to which they object. They might find the things you propose to do with their data, like training your AI models, is or will harm them or society at large by, for instance, manipulating them, having an undue influence on their decisions and actions because they feel they're being watched, miscategorizing them and so denying them a good or service they are worthy of (e.g., credit, housing, insurance, etc.), causing them emotional distress with how your

AI chooses to construct their social media or news feed, and on and on. In short, and at bottom, the expression of a concern about privacy in the context of AI is often the expression of a concern that your organization will engage in ethical misconduct by virtue of deploying ethically unsafe AI. Users want control over their data so you can't hurt them. In this way, talk of privacy is shorthand for AI ethics more generally.

Getting It Right

By this time, you should have a grip on the basics of AI, the foundations of ethics, and the three big challenges of AI ethics: bias, explainability, and privacy. And as a result of the Structure from Content Lessons, you should start to see a bit of an outline of an AI ethical risk program. Now it's time to really start throwing that Structure into relief, first by looking at how people usually attempt this and get it wrong. Then, I promise, I'll show you how to do it the right way.

Recap

- The two Structure from Content Lessons that relate to privacy and can guide approaches to Structure that are gleaned from understanding Content:
    - Before you start collecting data to train your AI, determine what ethical level of privacy is appropriate for the use case.

  - Your organization needs an individual or, ideally, a set of individuals, that can make responsible, expert-informed decisions when ethical values conflict.

- AI ethics invariably includes data ethics, insofar as machine learning requires the AI-developing or deploying organization to acquire or use troves of data.
  - This data, and more specifically, the ML it is used to train, is often built to make predictions about users, consumers, citizens, employees, and so on. These predictions, and the subsequent actions, may or may not have their best interests as their prime target, and people often insist, not unreasonably, that their privacy has been violated by virtue of the data collected and the kinds of predictions that were made.

- Privacy has three aspects:
  - Regulatory compliance
  - The integrity and security of data (cybersecurity)
  - Ethics

- Privacy is often equated with anonymity. While having personally identifiable information properly anonymized is important (and a responsibility from both an ethical and cybersecurity perspective), complaints about privacy violations extend far beyond a lack of anonymity.

- Privacy, in the context of AI ethics, is best understood as the extent to which people have knowledge and control over their data without undue pressure. Put differently, organizations' respect for privacy is, in large part, respect for the autonomy of the people whose data they collect and deploy their AI on.

- The four elements of the Five Ethical Levels of privacy are:
  - Transparency
  - Data control
  - Opt out by default
  - Full services
- The more of these elements that consumers are provided, the higher the level of privacy a company reaches. The Five Ethical Levels of Privacy based on these elements are, in order from least private to most private:
  - Level one: blindfolded and handcuffed. Only full services are provided to consumers.
  - Level two: handcuffed. Full services and transparency are provided.
  - Level three: pressured. Transparency and data control are provided.
  - Level four: slightly curtailed. Transparency, data control, and opt-out by default are provided.
  - Level five: trusting and grateful. All four elements are provided.
- Not every company in every product should strive for level five. Privacy is one value among many, and tradeoffs between it and other values have to be made in a way that respects an organization's more general ethical commitments and priorities.

A BRIEF INTERLUDE

You might be wondering what this is. It's not a chapter. It's not really about Content, and it's not quite Structure either. Let's call it a "philosophical interlude." A palate cleanser before we dive headlong into Structure. I want to say something about the title of this book.[1]

A common view is that tools (and machines) are ethically neutral; there's nothing intrinsically good or bad or right or wrong about, say, a screwdriver. All the ethics of screwdrivering come down to what you're screwing. Building houses for the needy? Good. Building concentration camps? Bad.

And tools don't—can't—get people to do things. They just sort of sit there, calling to no one and prompting no action.

The view that tools are ethically neutral is plausible, at least when applied to screwdrivers. Should we also think AI is ethically neutral? It's a tool, after all. You might think the ethics of AI just comes down to how you use it. Facial recognition for capturing really bad guys? Good. Facial recognition for tracking innocent civilians? Bad.

But we've already seen that things are more nuanced than that. Consider, for instance, the chapter on bias. We learned that *how you develop* AI bears on the features of the tool you've created. You make decisions on what training data set to use, what threshold and what objective function to set, what benchmark to test against, all of which bears on whether the outputs are discriminatory. It doesn't matter how the end user deploys it or, unlike with a screwdriver, whether they have good intentions. Using a discriminatory AI will force the user to discriminate when they use that AI, even if they're intending no harm.

Think also about what we learned about privacy. AI (and more specifically, machine learning) can only exist if it has lots of data to feed on. All else equal, the more data the better (as we saw in chapter 3). Thus, organizations that develop AI are highly incentivized to gather and use as much data as possible, which in turn incentivizes infringing on people's privacy to mine for that data. It's the nature of the machine learning beast to demand of those that want to unleash its power that they vacuum up all that data. Screwdrivers make no such demands.

There is no such thing as ethically neutral AI. The people who commission, design, develop, deploy, and approve an AI are quite unlike those who make screwdrivers. When you develop AI, you are developing ethical—or unethical—machines.

5

AI Ethics Statements That Actually Do Something

In chapter 1 we saw how ethics can be concrete in the sense that it's not mushy touchy-feely opinion, so let's everyone shrug their shoulders and move on. Ethical beliefs are about the world, specifically, about what is right and wrong, good and bad, permissible and impermissible, and organizations can get ethics right or wrong. In chapters 2 through 4, we dug into the details of three complex ethical issues in AI: bias, explainability, and privacy. Through an understanding of those issues, we learned a variety of Structure from Content Lessons.

All of this and more must ultimately coalesce into an AI ethical risk program: an articulation of how a Structure in your organization gets created, scaled, and maintained to systematically and comprehensively identify and manage the ethical, reputational, regulatory, and legal risks of AI. But if your organization is like most, you (justifiably) see this as a big lift. You're unlikely to put this book down and immediately get to work creating this program and the organizational and cultural change it entails.

Where to start, then? The standard first step in industry, among nonprofits, and even among countries, is to articulate ethical standards for AI development and deployment—a set of ethical values or principles. Sometimes they're referred to as "AI Ethics Principles," though increasingly, they're considered the organization's approach to "Responsible" or "Trustworthy" AI. Hundreds of organizations have put out such statements, and it's a fine place to start. Articulating ethical standards is obviously important if you want guidance for the board, the C-suite, product owners and developers, and so on. You've got to start somewhere.

It isn't necessary to dive into the details of any one particular AI ethics statement, for while the lists vary, just about all of them list a bunch of the following as their "principles" or "values":

- Fairness
- Antidiscrimination
- Transparency
- Explainability
- Respect
- Accountability
- Accuracy
- Security
- Reliability

- Safety
- Privacy
- Beneficence
- Human in the loop, human control, human oversight, human-centric design

The lists are usually accompanied with a sentence or two about what the organization means when it says it values these things. Here are some real-world examples:

- *Diversity, nondiscrimination, and fairness.* The BMW Group respects human dignity and therefore sets out to build fair AI applications. This includes preventing noncompliance by AI applications.[1]
- *Transparent.* We are transparent when a customer communicates with an AI and regarding our use of customer data.[2]
- *Data protection and privacy.* Data protection and privacy are a corporate requirement and at the core of every product and service.[3] We communicate clearly how, why, where, and when customer and anonymized user data is used in our AI software.[4]
- *Accountability.* We will design AI systems that provide appropriate opportunities for feedback, relevant explanations, and appeal. Our AI technologies will be subject to appropriate human direction and control.[5]

I said that this is a good place to start. But here as elsewhere, execution is everything, and in my estimation, this is all a bit weak.

The problem isn't that anything here is false or ethically problematic. It's that such statements aren't particularly *helpful* to an organization that is serious about integrating AI ethical risk mitigation standards into its AI ecosystem. I've had multiple companies reach out to me after they have "strong internal agreement on a set of AI ethics principles," which always look something like the above, but have hit a wall when it comes to putting those principles into practice. How do you get from a statement to answering questions like, "Do we need an ethics committee?" "Should we tell our product developers to engage in 'AI ethics by design'?" and ultimately, and always, "How do we turn this into key performance indicators (KPIs)?!"

But a move now to talk about structure, process, and practice, is too soon. These companies are running into trouble because these kinds of lists—sometimes couched in the comforting corporate language of "frameworks"—suffer from a number of problems that prevent them from being helpful.

Four Problems with Standard AI Ethics Statements

1. They lump together Content and Structure

The distinction between Content and Structure roughly maps to the distinction between goals and strategies or tactics, and if you can't distinguish between goals and strategies, not only are you confused, but you're going to make bad decisions that lead to bad outcomes. You might, for instance, sacrifice a goal for a strategy because you don't have a firm grip on these things to begin with.

Take "accountability," for instance. It appears on almost everyone's list. But being accountable or, rather, ensuring that particular people in product development and deployment are accountable for your AI's impacts isn't an ethical goal in itself. It's a strategy to reach a different goal, which is to increase the probability you'll deploy ethical AI. Making particular people accountable—by, say, assigning role-specific responsibilities—is a way to decrease the probability that things will fall between the cracks. And if you *could* somehow stop things from falling between the cracks and that method worked without holding anyone accountable, then you could stop holding people accountable. (Of course, there probably is no such thing, but the thought experiment demonstrates that accountability is a strategy, not a goal.)

2. They lump together ethical and nonethical values

When you're talking AI ethics, the values and principles you stand behind should be ethical in nature. But these lists include nonethical values.

Take, for instance, security and accuracy. The former refers to the domain of security for the sake of preventing and defending against various kinds of cyberattacks. The latter refers to the goals of engineers training the AI models.

Including these things is commensurate with the slide I noted earlier, from talking about "AI ethics" to "Responsible" or "Trustworthy" AI. In principle, this is fine. In practice, it tends to push ethical concerns into the back seat. Here's how a lot of conversations that I've had go:

"Do you have an AI ethical risk program?"

"Oh yes, we take responsible AI very seriously."

"That's great! What are you doing around it?"

"Well, we do a lot of testing and monitoring of our models, checking for data drift, overfitting, and so on. We've built security into the product development process, and we make sure our model outputs are explainable."

"I see. So when it comes to AI ethics in particular, what are you doing?"

"AI ethics specifically? Um . . . I guess it's just the explainability stuff, really."

"Got it. So it sounds like your Responsible AI Program is primarily about how well your model functions from an engineering and security perspective, without a particular focus on, say, discriminatory outputs, privacy violations, and various ethical and reputational risks that can be realized in particular use cases with AI."

"Yeah, I guess that's right. We're not really sure what to do with that stuff."

The problem isn't with a concept like "Responsible AI" or "Trustworthy AI." And it's absolutely essential for organizations to earn trust that they protect their AI models, the data they train on, and the data they output, from cyberattacks as well as for their developers to create accurate models and reliable products. The problem is that lumping together ethical, cybersecurity, and engineering issues into one pile of responsible development and deployment affects how people think and make decisions about where they are and where they need to be in their AI ethical risk journey. If we don't lump them together, but instead talk about them as distinct entities that need to be individually addressed, people will address each of them instead of not realizing that their high score on their Responsible AI metrics is primarily the result of overperforming on engineering metrics, not the result of (underperforming) ethical risk mitigation efforts.

Another pragmatic difficulty here is that, insofar as an AI Ethics Statement is the start of a more general AI ethical risk program, and it's deployed effectively (more on this later), some senior member of the organization will have to own this program. That senior member will have authority over those people who ensure that the values are being operationalized. But it is rare for a single senior leader to own AI ethics *and* AI cybersecurity *and* AI engineering or product development. As a result, it makes for a more functional document if it speaks to a cohesive program for which a senior leader can be responsible. It should go without saying—or rather, it should be said elsewhere—that a senior leader like a chief information and security officer should work to protect their AI infrastructure against attack and that the chief data officer should work to ensure accurate and reliable models.

3. They lump together instrumental and noninstrumental values

When something is of instrumental value, it's good because it gets you something else that's good. Pens are of instrumental value because they help you to write things down, which is good for remembering things, which is good for getting things done you want to get done. Being famous has instrumental value because it allows you to get reservations at fancy restaurants. Voting has instrumental value because it's a good way for the will of the people to be expressed and have a significant impact on how they will be governed. And so on.

Noninstrumental value is . . . well, it's what it sounds like.

Things that are of noninstrumental value are good in themselves, good for their own sakes, intrinsically good, and so on. What is noninstrumentally valuable? Ethicists disagree, but pleasure and pain are good candidates ("Why is pleasure good? Why is pain bad? I don't know . . . they just are!"), as are happiness, a meaningful life, justice, and autonomy.

The relationship between instrumental and noninstrumental values is pretty clear: the noninstrumental values explain why these other things are of instrumental value. For example, we instrumentally value exercise because it is conducive to health. Health itself is also of instrumental value because it helps us to avoid sickness, which is painful. Why do we want to avoid the pain of sickness? Well, it's not because it gets us some further thing. Rather, it's just something we noninstrumentally disvalue.[6] That said, some things are both instrumentally and noninstrumentally valuable. For example, living a great life is noninstrumentally valuable, and it's instrumentally valuable because it inspires other people to lead great lives.

The distinction is important if we're going to think clearly about the content of our AI ethical values. In particular, we don't want to sacrifice what's of noninstrumental value for something of instrumental value; that would usually be both ethically problematic and just kind of a boneheaded thing to do. Unfortunately, I'm afraid those standard AI ethics statements do it quite often. Consider, for instance:

- Human in the loop, human-centric design, human oversight
- Transparency
- Explainability

Human in the loop. Having a human in the loop means that you have a human decision-maker standing between the outputs of an AI and the impactful decision that gets made. For instance, if the AI says, "Fire (on) that person," you want a human taking that into consideration in deciding what to do and you don't want the AI to automatically fire (on) that person. But why do you want a human in the loop? Presumably because you think having that kind of human (emotionally) intelligent, experienced oversight is important for preventing really bad outcomes. In other words, that person plays a certain *function*—to stop some bad things from happening when the AI goes awry. They are of *instrumental* value, at least in some cases, and having a human in the loop is not a goal all by itself. So, it would be odd to say that one of your values is having a human in the loop.

Think about what would happen if we found a method of AI oversight that was better than a human in the loop. Suppose, for instance, you had one AI that checks the outputs of another AI. And suppose the overseer AI were better at overseeing than a human (because, for instance, the human is too slow to keep up with the outputs of the AI being overseen). It would be counterproductive to your goal of ensuring, as best you can, ethically safe outputs to stick with the human over the superior AI. The danger in claiming that having a human in the loop is one of your values is that you might make that decision because you've confused a goal—ethical safety—with a strategy for attaining that goal, having a human in the loop.

Transparency. Transparency is about how openly and honestly you communicate with others, including, say, how clearly you communicate to users of your AI what data it collects, what the organization might do with that data, and the very fact that they're engaging with an AI in the first place. Is being transparent an instrumental or noninstrumental value? Does it lead to good outcomes or is it good in itself?

As I see things, transparency is of instrumental value.

Transparency is part of a strategy to gain trust *because you're trustworthy*. Since acting ethically earns trust, and acting unethically destroys it, ensuring that your AI is deployed ethically is crucial to an overall effort to earn trust.

Your goal cannot simply be to get trust. Con men are very good at getting people's trust. Being highly manipulative is compatible with getting people's trust. But the fact that you can get people's trust through nefarious means doesn't make you trustworthy. What's more, it's a highly unstable situation; even if you can get away with it for some time, eventually you'll get found out. Grifters are nomadic for a reason.

Notice that being trustworthy is not enough to get trust. You also need to communicate to people what it is you are doing or they won't know that what you're doing makes you trustworthy. In other words, first get your ethical house in order. That will make you trustworthy. Now tell everyone about your house. That will get you the trust, but not because you've been manipulative. Transparency is good because it builds trust—it's a *means to the end* of building trust—on the condition that you're behaving in a way that warrants or earns trust.[7]

Explainability. Sometimes explainability matters, as we saw in chapter 3, because it's required for expressing respect. That's a case of regarding an explanation as an expression of a noninstrumental value. In other cases, however, it's ethically permissible either to not provide any explanation at all (e.g., in cases of informed consent to using a black box) or to provide an explanation solely because it's useful to do so (e.g., in cases of identifying bias or because it makes the product usable by consumers).

While it makes sense to list "respect" as a value and, in some cases, to fill it in with the conditions under which explanations are required to express that respect, it doesn't make a whole lot of sense to list "explainability" as a value. After all, if your statement articulates your values or principles that you don't want to breach, but explainability is only sometimes important, either you'll have to live up to silly standards of making everything explainable or you'll have to be in breach of your stated principles whenever you reasonably don't prioritize explainability for a given model. In short, it would be silly to include it in a list of values, potentially dangerous insofar as you sacrifice some other goal on its behalf unnecessarily (e.g., sacrificing near-perfect accuracy of a cancer-diagnosing AI), and also tremendously inefficient, because you'll spend many hours working on explaining something for which we don't need an explanation.

4. They describe overly abstract values

The fourth problem with the standard approach is its most significant: these principles don't actually tell anyone *what to do.*

My favorite example of this is the value of fairness. It's on everyone's list. No one wants to have unfair AI. And that, really, is the problem. The value of "fairness" is so broad that even the Ku Klux Klan subscribes to it. Ask a Klan member, "Hey, are you for fairness? Do you value justice?" You'll hear in reply, "Absolutely!" Of course, their conception of what counts as fair and just widely differs from what your organization counts as fair and just (one hopes). But the fact that everyone can subscribe to it is enough to show that it doesn't actually indicate anything about what to do.

The same can be said of most other values. (Google, for instance, proudly proclaims as one of its AI ethics principles "being socially beneficial." What benefits should be conferred to whom, to what extent, and for how long or often is, to an ethicist's eye, an absence with a presence.) And we can see how trivial they are when we see what sorts of questions remain. Here are just a few.

- What counts as a violation of privacy?
  - Maybe my AI gathers a ton of data from hundreds of thousands of people, including Bob, anonymizes that data, and then trains an ML in a way that Bob never knows his data was used in this way. Further, no individual person knows about Bob, since it's all in a massive data set. Have I violated Bob's privacy? What if Bob clicked "I accept" on the banner that links to Terms and Conditions that explains all that in legalese? Is that consent, from an ethical perspective?
- What does respecting someone look like in product design?
  - Should we go with "buyer beware" or "we've got your back"? Is it assuming that people are autonomous rational agents capable of free choice even in the face of enticements? Or is it a matter of thinking that some product design choices create a kind of enticement that undermines autonomy and so we should forbid those design choices?

- When does something count as discriminatory?
  - In chapter 2, we saw the way in which this question is complicated and gives rise to a host of others: When is differential impact across subpopulations ethically acceptable? How do we assess which of the various metrics for fairness is appropriate in a given use case? How do we approach given current antidiscrimination law?

Put plainly: if you want your values to be nontrivial and action guiding, you'll have to do more than mouth words like "fairness," "privacy," and "respect."

Better Content Guides Actions

We want to integrate ethical risk mitigation standards into AI product development and deployment, and we need an ethical North Star, some place to start the journey of nestling ethical standards into operations. Typically, people articulate a set of values like the ones listed above and ask, "How do we operationalize this?" Then, they hit a dead end because of a lack of clarity (the three lumps) and a lack of substance (overly abstract values). We can fix this. We need to keep Content and Structure separate, keep our ethics distinct from our nonethics, and articulate our values in a concrete way.

Here are four steps you can take to accomplish exactly that.

Step 1. State your values by thinking about your ethical nightmares

Let's remember that we're engaged in AI ethical *risk mitigation.* We are not, at least not first and foremost, in the business of striving toward some rosy ideal. That said, sometimes a good defense is a good offense, and it makes sense to articulate your goals in a positive light: we express the values we're striving for instead of the disvalues we're trying to avoid. But you can articulate those values in light of the ethical nightmares you want to avoid.

Your ethical nightmares are partly informed by the industry you're in, the particular kind of organization you are, and the kinds of relationships you need to have with your clients, customers, and other stakeholders for things to go well. Take three examples to see how this might go:

- If you're a health-care provider that, among other things, uses AI to make treatment recommendations to doctors and nurses, and widespread false positives and false negatives in testing for (life-threatening) illnesses is your ethical nightmare, then doing no harm is your value.

- If you're a financial services company that uses AI to give investment recommendations and clients being (and feeling) taken advantage of is one of your ethical nightmares, then clear, honest, comprehensive communication is one of your values.

- If you're a social media platform that facilitates communications of various sorts among hundreds of millions of people around the globe and misinformation and lies spreading in a way that potentially undermines democracy is one of your ethical nightmares, then the communication of (reasonably thought) true claims is one of your values.

Notice how specific nightmares give rise to values that are more clearly defined than highly abstract values like respect, fairness, and transparency. In the case of financial services, we could have simply said, "Respect our clients." But *ethical nightmares involving a breach of respect* brings things into focus. Those ethical nightmares highlight *the ways in which* an organization may fail to respect someone. And by giving substance to the ways in which you might fail to respect them, you can say more about what, for your organization, respect *is*. Respect is, at least in part, engaging in clear, honest, and comprehensive communications about one's recommendations. It's about telling the truth, the whole truth, and nothing but the truth.

Step 2: Explain why you value what you do in a way that connects to your organization's mission or purpose

If you can't do this, then it seems like ethical goals or nightmares are just something bolted onto an already finished product. If you're going to weave ethical risk mitigation standards throughout your AI strategy and product life cycle, all of which is done for the sake of the organization's mission, then you need to show how your ethical values are part and parcel of achieving that mission. If you can't do that, then employees will regard it as a nice to have, not a need to have, and you'll see the AI ethics program fall by the wayside and your ethical risks realized. Here's what it might look like to weld your mission to your ethical values:

- We are, first and foremost, health-care providers. We are entrusted with one of the most sacred things on this planet: human life. More specifically, each and every one of our patients trusts us to take the best care of them that we possibly can. While speed and scale are important, it can never come at the cost of decreased quality of care.

- We are financial professionals. People give us their money so that we can protect and grow their wealth. This is money they or their loved ones have worked hard to acquire. This is money for their children's school and daycare. This is money for their retirement. This is money for life-saving surgeries. This is money for family vacations or a once-in-a-lifetime world tour. Our clients have given us control over the necessary means to live a life they find worth living. The last thing we can do is betray that trust. They must never feel they are being taken advantage of by people with more knowledge than them about how the complicated world of finance works. We must be diligent, not only in our investment recommendations for them, but in our communications with them about those recommendations.

- We are a platform that facilitates connections and conversations among hundreds of millions of people. Sometimes those communications are wonderful or at least benign. Other times, it is propaganda, lies, and other deceptions that can have disastrous consequences. Insofar as we enable those kinds of communications, we play a crucial role in what people come to believe about the world around them, which informs what they do. We cannot pretend we have nothing to do with these things because the communications are not coming out of our mouths. We are putting those communications in front of people. It's our responsibility not to put lies in front of them. Not only do we owe our individual users that protection, but we also owe society as a whole that we will not play a role in its deterioration. We have already seen what can happen when disinformation routinely goes viral, and we cannot abide those consequences.

Step 3: Connect your values to what you take to be ethically impermissible

It's one thing to say you value something. But if that statement is to have substance, it must be connected to an articulation of what courses of action are off the table. Values provide, at a minimum, the guardrails of ethical permissibility. You need to say what those guardrails are in as concrete a way as you can. For example:

- *Doing no harm.* We will never use an AI to make recommendations that do not consistently outperform our best doctors.
- *Clear, honest, comprehensive communication.* We will always communicate in a way that is clear and easily digestible. This means, for instance, that we will not communicate information that a reasonable person may deem important through, for instance, long text-filled documents written with a lot of jargon. We will ensure that people will know what they need to know when they need to know it, and we'll even remind them of that information either when appropriate or at regular intervals. In some cases, we'll go so far as to give our clients quizzes to ensure that they've understood what we've told them.

- *Communication of (reasonably thought) true claims.* We will flag all posts that appear to be going viral. By "appear to be going viral," we mean any post that is shared or viewed at a rate of *x* shares or views per minute. When a post is flagged, we will cap the rate at which the post can be shared at *y* shares or views per minute, and that post will be viewed by at least two people to determine whether it contains misinformation and, if so, the probability of people being wronged if that misinformation is believed by *z* percent of viewers of that content. In that event, we will freeze sharing of that content or take down the post. Further, if a person posts such content more than *x* times per week, that person's account will be frozen for *y* weeks. A second offense will lead to a *z*-year ban, and a third offense will lead to a permanent ban.

Step 4: Articulate how you will realize your ethical goals or avoid your ethical nightmares

Now that we know what you value, how it ties into your organizational mission, and what things are off-limits, you need to say something about how you're going to make all of this happen. The goal here is not to be exhaustive. It is to take your best attempt at articulating the Structure you'll put in place. For example:

- *Accountable.* We will take concrete steps to build organizational awareness around these issues, for instance, by educating our people when onboarding new employees, with seminars, workshops, and other educational and upskilling tools. We will also assign role-specific responsibilities, the discharging of which is relevant to bonuses, raises, and promotions, to all employees involved in the development, procurement, or deployment of AI products, whether those products are used internally or in the service of our clients. A senior executive will be responsible for growing our AI ethics program, including tracking progress against our goals using publicly available KPIs.

- *Due diligence process.* We will systematically engage in rigorous ethical risk analyses throughout production and procurement of AI.
- *Monitoring.* We will monitor the impacts of our products with an eye toward discovering their unintended consequences.

This is still fairly high level, of course. We haven't said anything about the content of those role-specific responsibilities, which senior executive will drive the program and what KPIs they may use to track progress, who will engage in the due diligence and monitoring procedures, and so on. Still, we know in broad outline the kinds of things that are already committed to.

We can now see a subset of an AI ethics statement from the organizations I've given as examples. Let's put it all together for one of them—the financial company—so we can see what things look like.

[Your value]: Clear, honest, and comprehensive communication

- **Why [you have that value].** We are financial professionals. People give us their money so that we can protect and grow their wealth. This is money they or their loved ones have worked hard to acquire. This is money for their children's school and daycare. This is money for their retirement. This is money for life-saving surgeries. This is money for family vacations or a once-in-a-lifetime world tour. Our clients have given us control over the necessary means to live a life they find worth living. The last thing we can do is betray that trust. They must never feel they are being taken advantage of by people with more knowledge than them about how the complicated world of finance works. We must be diligent, not only in our investment recommendations for them, but in our communications with them about those recommendations.
- **What [you do because you value this].** We will always communicate in a way that is clear and easily digestible. This means, for instance, that we will not communicate information that a not unreasonable person may deem important through, for instance, long textual documents written with a lot of jargon. We will ensure that people will know what they need to know when they need to know it, and we'll even remind them of that information either when appropriate or at regular intervals. In some cases, we'll go so far as to give our clients quizzes to ensure that they've understood what we've told them.

- **How [you ensure you will do what you say you will do].** We will take concrete steps to build organizational awareness around this issue, for instance, by educating our people when onboarding new employees, with seminars, workshops, and other educational and upskilling tools. We will also assign role-specific responsibilities, the discharging of which is relevant to bonuses, raises, and promotions, to all employees involved in the development, procurement, or deployment of AI products, whether those products are used internally or in the service of our clients. A senior executive will be responsible for growing our AI ethics program, including tracking progress against our goals using publicly available KPIs.

The value, the why, and the what are all specific to the ethical nightmare of this particular financial services company. The how isn't specific to it, but it's nonetheless crucial to specify to internal and external stakeholders that there is thought behind how your goals are going to be achieved.

Advantages to Creating Your Ethical North Star This Way

When your AI ethics statement, principles, values, framework, or whatever you want to call it dives deep on Content in this way, you create numerous advantages.

First, you've defined goals and strategies, which enables you to talk tactics and, in some cases, to take action. You've articulated the Content in a way that connects it to what is ethically off-limits. And you already have some idea about how to operationalize this. It's certainly no great mystery, as it would be had you said, "We respect our clients and we always act with integrity." No clear marching orders there. But "we will always communicate in a way that is clear and easily digestible" gives you something to do: before sending out communications, and when programming your AI to communicate information to your clients, check to ensure that it is easily intelligible and digestible. When should you do this and exactly how should you do it? That will depend on the particulars of your organization and will come out when we start building the customized requisite Structure for achieving your ethical goals. But at least now we know what we're trying to achieve.

In fact—brace yourself—KPIs are beginning to take shape. Suppose you have a survey that asks your end users how intelligible and digestible they find your communications (though don't use that language). You can ask test groups how intelligible and digestible they find the communications. Suppose you use an AI to check the reading proficiency grade level required to understand the text. All of these have what people love: numbers to track. And we got there by thinking seriously about Content.

Second, now that you've specified your values, you can perform a gap analysis of where your company is relative to where you want it to be. This includes a review of current infrastructure, policies, processes, and people.

Third, if the process by which these values are articulated sufficiently includes members from across the organization—not just cross-functionally across the C-suite but also including more junior members of the organization—you will create organizational awareness and get insights from a diverse array of people, including people of different skill sets, knowledge bases, interests, experiences, and demographics. What is particularly important here is that when you ask people for their help and listen to them, and make changes in light of their feedback, you get their *justified* buy-in. This is far better than compliance to a set of principles cast down from atop Mount Olympus. These are people who rightly feel they've played a part in shaping these values and so feel ownership of the AI ethics program.

Fourth, by articulating what is ethically impermissible and explaining why it is impermissible, you've given people a crucial tool for thinking about the ethically tough cases: where it's not quite clear whether some decision or action or product contravenes the organization's AI ethical values. We'll talk more about this when we discuss ethics committees, but for now we only need to notice that explanations for why some things are impermissible and why the organization does X are helpful in deciding cases where it's difficult to discern the right thing to do.

Last, while this document can be used internally as an AI ethics North Star, you can also use it as a public-facing document for the purposes of branding and public relations. Insofar as the document is far more specific than generic statements of values, it's more credible. Be warned, though: writing this document and sharing it with your organization or anyone outside the organization is a big commitment. It's a promise. And if you break that promise, there's no telling how much trust you'll lose.

Intent on keeping that promise? We'll see how in the next chapter.

Recap

- Standard approaches to creating AI ethical North Stars suffer from four problems:
  - Lumping together Content and Structure
  - Lumping together ethical with nonethical values
  - Lumping together instrumental and noninstrumental values
  - Articulating values too abstractly to guide action
- A better approach consists of four steps:
  - Step 1: State your values by thinking about your ethical nightmares, where those nightmares are partly informed by the industry you're in, the particular kind of organization you are, and the kinds of relationships you need to have with your clients, customers, and other stakeholders for things to go well.
  - Step 2: Explain why you value what you do in a way that connects it to your organization's mission or purpose.
  - Step 3: Connect your values to what you take to be ethically impermissible.
  - Step 4: Articulate, at a high level, how you will realize your ethical goals or avoid your ethical nightmares.

- That better approach has five advantages:
  - It provides you with clearly defined goals and strategies, and does so in a way that determining KPIs is not far off.
  - You can now perform a gap analysis of your organization in light of these ethical values.
  - If done right, you'll get insights from across the organization, create organizational awareness, and earn organizational buy-in.
  - You'll have created a tool that will help you think through the tough ethical cases.
  - You've created a credible document for branding and PR purposes.

6

Conclusions Executives Should Come To

An AI ethics statement is a nice start. It's also the tip of the iceberg.

Every time you find a use case for AI, your organization faces a host of ethical questions. Those include some with which we're already familiar:

- Which of these incompatible metrics for bias are ethically appropriate?
- What is the most effective bias-mitigation strategy?
- Is explainability important and, if so, how important is it relative to accuracy?
- Are the rules the AI has discovered for turning inputs into outputs good, reasonable, just, fair?
- What level of privacy should we aim for?

Ethical risk issues pertaining to bias, explainability, and privacy, however, are only a subset of all ethical risks and opportunities your organization faces when using AI. Different use cases entail different sets of ethical risks. Your organization will also face questions like these:

- Is this foisting an undue burden on our users?
- Will this business model for our AI result in ethically objectionable (wealth) inequality?
- Does this AI encourage us or our users to be manipulative?
- Is it our responsibility to fix this problem? Shouldn't that be up to our client?
- We developed the model for X, but is it also ethically permissible to use it for Y?
- Does using this software when hiring people communicate a lack of respect (e.g., sentiment analysis)?
- How transparent should we be about when we're using AI and how much we're using it?
- Do we need a person between the model outputs and the action taken on the person the AI is making a "decision" about or can it be fully automated?
- Are there particular AI ethical risks we need to pay special attention to, given our industry and the particular kind of organization we are?

You're a senior executive at an organization that either is or is about to develop, procure, and deploy AI. By now, you're probably thinking, *How the hell are we going to handle all these questions?* After some time contemplating the issue and discussing it with others, you should come to the following seven conclusions.

1. We're going to have to get crystal clear on what our AI ethical standards are.

2. We're going to have to make our data scientists, engineers, and product owners aware of these issues. In fact, everyone in our organization who might develop, procure, or deploy AI needs to be aware, including those in HR, marketing, strategy, and so on. This will require not only training, but also developing a culture in which that training gets uptake.

3. We need to provide our product development teams with tools to help them think about the ethical risks of the products they're working on. We also need clear processes and practices to which both product development teams and procurement personnel must adhere.

4. At the same time, we must realize that these issues are complex, and while standard processes and practices and tools are helpful, they are only a first line of defense. To seriously address the ethical, reputational, regulatory, and legal risks, we need the experts in the room. Product teams need either to include such experts or, more likely, to elevate issues to the relevant experts.

5. Staff needs to be held accountable for using these tools and complying with these processes on pain of penalties ranging from lack of bonuses, to inability to be promoted, to firing. Relatedly, we need to financially incentivize taking these

issues seriously or at least not provide financial incentives in such a way that they are motivated to deprioritize ethical risks.

6. We need to do all of this in a way such that we can track both the extent to which the organization is adopting these new standards and the extent to which meeting those standards identifies and mitigates the risks those standards are aimed at addressing. We need a clearly articulated AI ethical risk program with KPIs.

7. A member of the C-suite needs to own all this. That person should be responsible for overseeing the creation, rollout, and maintenance of our AI ethical risk program.

Making sure these seven things happen is *how* you're going to identify and mitigate AI ethical risks. It's your AI ethical risk program. It's your Structure.

Let's dive deeper into each one of these conclusions. It's straightforward at a high level, but here as elsewhere, the devil is in the details.

1. AI Ethical Standards

Let's suppose you have an AI ethics statement generated in line with the recommendations of the previous chapter. It's robust. It ties articulations of your values to what your organization considers off-limits. But between "never do this" and "always do that," there is a lot of "maybe do this." And your organization needs a way of tackling those issues. To be sure, the ethics statement, if sufficiently robust, is an aid in such matters. But you can take another big step forward by thinking about the tough cases before they happen.

In both law and ethics, there are gray areas. Cases in which it may be legally permissible, but it's not clear because there are laws that, on the face of it, conflict. Cases in which it may be ethically permissible, but it's not obvious, because there are ethical considerations pointing in opposite directions (e.g., the rights of a few people versus the good of a great many). The legal or ethical principles, by themselves, don't provide clear guidance.

Deliberations on tough cases in both arenas standardly rely on reasoning by way of analogy from other cases where there is already some reasonable judgment made. Lawyers will depend on case law to help them see the way. For instance, if self-defense is sufficient legal justification for killing in this case, as the courts determined it is, then arguably it's sufficient in this new kind of case, which is a bit different but sufficiently similar to warrant the same conclusion. The Supreme Court of the United States is (ideally) guided in just this way; its deliberations consist, at least in part, in considering existing case law, which is meant to aid in the proper interpretation and application of the law.

Ethicists engage in the same kind of deliberations. If you're ethically required to save this person in this circumstance, then it seems you're also ethically required to save this other person in this other circumstance; the cases are slightly different, but they're sufficiently similar to warrant the same conclusion.

When your organization is dealing with tough AI ethical risk cases, you would do well to appeal to "ethical case law." Of course, you can't use legal case law, since we're dealing with AI ethical risks, which overlaps with, but is not identical to, AI legal risks.

However, you can create your own ethical case law that is tailored not only to your industry but also to your organization.

Details can vary around how you go about doing this, but the short of it requires using real cases your organization has faced in the past (or cases other sufficiently similar companies have faced) or fictional examples you think could quite possibly become real in the not-to-distant future. You can then ask such general questions as "Would deploying that AI be compatible with our AI ethical commitments?" and, "What would we tell a client who asked us to develop that AI?" You can also ask more specific questions, like "In this imagined use case for this imagined AI, what metric for fairness would be appropriate?" or "How important is explainability for this product?" or "What ethical level of privacy should we aim to reach in the development of this AI?" And in all such cases, you'll want to spell out *why* you came to the conclusion you did. That is precisely the kind of reasoning and conclusions you'll want to appeal to when it's time for the real deal.

Getting started on this is actually quite simple. When I work with clients to write an AI ethics statement, one exercise we engage in involves members of their team giving thumbs up or thumbs down in response to various statements I put before them. "We will never sell your data to a third party," for instance. "We will always engage in a robust ethical due diligence process when developing our models," goes another. Or, "There is certain information we will not collect or attempt to infer about our subscribers (e.g., political affiliation, sexual preferences, and so on)."

While there is consensus or near consensus in response to many of the statements, which in turn lands them in the AI Ethics Statement, there are invariably a number of statements on which the team is split. "Well, maybe in this case," says one member, "but not in the other." Or, "Well I'm not sure what would happen if our client asked us to do that. Maybe we would? Do we kind of do that already?"

Those are statements that generally don't go into the AI Ethics Statement because they are simply too controversial. Nonetheless, at some point those tough questions will come knocking on the door. That's why I take those statements about which there's disagreement, work through that disagreement—untangling objections and counter-objections, clarifying relevant ethical concepts and issues so confusion doesn't win the day, pinning down the exact reasoning for a decision, and so on. When we're done, we've taken a huge step in creating that organization's ethical case law.

You might wonder why you can't just wait to engage in those deliberations when it's real life. Why not just wait until the question is at your doorstep and handle it then? There are two reasons.

First, there's a difference between tackling the tough questions and tackling the tough questions *well*. Thinking through these cases efficiently, with a clear head, and effectively, is a *skill* that needs to be developed. A muscle to be exercised. Asking why you can't just wait until you actually face an ethical challenge is like an athlete asking why they have to train before a competition.

Second, ethical deliberation can be compromised for a number of reasons. Aristotle noted that our addiction to pleasure and our abhorrence of pain often leads us to engage in muddled thinking on ethical matters.[1] We conclude that we shouldn't do X because it's the *wrong* thing to do, when really X is the *right but painful thing* to do. Our aversion to pain leads to self-deception and rationalizations. The corporate equivalent to pain and pleasure is profit and loss (and at the individual level, promotions and raises), which muddles our ethical thought. We conclude that deploying this AI is ethically permissible when really deploying it is impermissible by our own ethical standards. We let a desire (profit, bonus, promotion, or just to be done with this project already) fool us into thinking we stand on steady ethical ground.

When we're creating our ethical case law, money isn't immediately held up before us. The heat of desire that Aristotle referenced isn't there to cloud our judgment. We can reflect in the cool hours when our eyes are not blinded by cartoonish dollar signs.

The ethical case law you create can be used in a variety of ways by a variety of people. Your product teams can use it as they develop AI. The experts (referenced in the fifth conclusion) and senior executives (as referenced in the seventh conclusion) can use it when they are tackling tough cases. And teams in charge of communicating, training, and upskilling your AI ethical standards to the organization as a whole can use it. The more robust your AI ethics statement and your ethical case law, the easier and more efficient it is to see and be guided by your organization's ethical North Star.

2. Organizational Awareness

Many executives assume that AI ethics is for the techies to figure out. We've already dispelled that notion; AI ethical risks do not admit of technical solutions. Another common assumption is that AI ethics is really just *for* techies and product teams generally. It's not an HR issue, or a marketing issue, or any other department, for that matter. We need to dispel this as well.

I have continually referenced the AI ethical risks that threaten your organization as a result of developing and *procuring* AI. Who procures AI? Increasingly, every department in your organization. There is, for instance, an explosion of AI vendors in HR, and their salespeople are in your HR people's inbox right now. The same goes for advertising and marketing. The general proliferation of AI means that AI is applied to every industry and every department in an organization.

Does your head of HR know about Amazon's biased hiring AI? Do they know how it happened? Do they know how bias can creep into an AI? Do they know the ethical, reputational, and legal implications of using biased AI? Does your chief medical officer know Optum's AI recommended paying more attention to white patients than to sicker Black patients? Are your doctors and nurses familiar with it? Does your advertising agency know about Facebook's AI that advertised houses for sale to white people and houses for rent to Black people?

These, and more, are things they need to know. They need to understand the potential risks built into a vendor's proposed solution. If they're unaware, then they won't ask the right questions during their due diligence. Users of the deployed software won't know to look out for unacceptable outcomes of a certain stripe. Your head of procurement will have a hell of a time on the witness stand when asked how your organization vets for the risks of AI that have been well documented and widely publicized.

AI ethics is not simply about what your product teams do. As AI gets integrated into every facet of an organization, the personnel in those facets need to be aware of these new sources of ethical risk. This will require a good deal of education and upskilling. It will also require new processes by which vendor software is vetted by appropriate personnel. If your HR department doesn't have that capacity internally, it will have to work with other departments that do.

3. Teams, Tools, and Processes

Your product development teams need not only knowledge about the issues and how, in principle, they can address them, but also concrete tools and processes for diligently carrying out ethical risk identification and mitigation. They need to engage in "AI ethics by design." There's so much to say here, it deserves its own chapter . . . right after this one.

4. Expert Oversight

Notwithstanding the coming chapter on tools and processes for product teams, I must stress that it would be unwise and unfair to place the burden of identifying and mitigating the ethical risks of AI primarily on the shoulders of data scientists, engineers, and product designers or owners.

It's unwise in that you're betting the reputation of your brand on the efficacy of these tools and your tech or design team to wield them sufficiently well. Keep in mind that one of the great appeals of AI is how quickly it scales. It's *built* to do big things. This means that when you have an ethical issue, it's never a small, localized mishap. You discriminate at scale. You apply unfair rules at scale. You violate privacy at scale. And so on. Given the complexity and difficulty of ethical issues that need to be countenanced—a few of which are captured at the start of this chapter—it's negligent to place the burden on the shoulders of people who lack expertise in ethics.

For similar reasons, it's unfair to expect data scientists, engineers, and product owners to do the kind of work for which they lack deep expertise. You have them making decisions on complex ethical, social, and political issues, all of which court reputational, regulatory, and legal risks that they are not equipped to handle and for which they cannot be made equipped in short (or even long) order.

A comparison with the health-care industry is helpful. In the wake of ethically horrific experiments—most infamously, perhaps, the Tuskegee experiments, in which doctors withheld penicillin from syphilitic Black people so they could observe the disease's unmitigated progression—the industry realized it needed ethical standards built into its operations, both in research and in how it treats patients. The first major step in the right direction consisted of the *Belmont Report*, which articulated the ethical standards by which the industry was to live and whose principles still loom large today: justice, respect for persons, and beneficence. A second major step consisted of educating medical researchers and practitioners about the ethical standards. Codes of conduct were developed, as were various processes to ensure patients were respected, for example, requiring informed consent before administering treatment. And third, medical researchers were required, by regulations, to attain institutional review board (IRB) approval. The idea there was clear: while having well-intentioned and educated researchers is great, it is not enough. To ensure the comprehensive identification and mitigation of ethical risks, researchers need to consult the appropriate experts, both because of their independence from the researching team and because of their capacity to see what researchers cannot.

The idea that AI researchers and practitioners can comprehensively and systematically identify and mitigate ethical risks using a set of tools and processes, in a way that medical researchers and practitioners cannot, is preposterous on its face. The right experts are needed to provide proper oversight. In fact, if you look back on the nine Structure from Content Lessons in chapters 2 through 4 (restated in the sidebar), you'll notice that *every single one of them is about getting the right experts involved.*

Structure from Content Lessons

When addressing the big three challenges of ethical AI, lessons on how to structure your approach emerge from the content of those challenges. In chapters 2 through 4, we identified nine such lessons.

Lessons Focused on Bias

- There must be an individual or set of individuals with expertise who determine which metrics of fairness are appropriate for the particular use case.
- You need an individual or set of individuals who have the relevant expertise for choosing bias-mitigation strategies.
- Identifying and mitigating biases of your models should start before training your model and, ideally, before determining your training data sets.
- You should include a lawyer when determining bias-mitigation techniques.

Lessons Focused on Explainability

- You need the right people to determine whether people or machine explanations are important for a given use case.
- In cases in which it's important to articulate the rules for how inputs are turned into outputs, you should include people with ethical and legal expertise to assess the fairness of the rules.
- Consult the end users of the AI software to determine whether an explanation is needed and what a good explanation looks like given their knowledge, skills, and purposes.

Lessons Focused on Privacy

- Before you start collecting data to train your AI, determine what ethical level of privacy is appropriate for the use case.
- There must be an individual or set of individuals who can make responsible, expert-informed decisions when ethical values conflict.

Any organization that is serious about AI ethical risks needs something that plays a role akin to that of an IRB. We can call it an AI IRB, or an AI Ethics Committee, or an AI Risk Board—the name matters far less than a determination of its function and powers. Further, that board can be a new entity within your organization, or it can be a set of responsibilities conferred upon an existing body, and depending on the size of your organization, you can have more than one. At a high level, its function is simple: to play an oversight role in systematically and comprehensively identifying and mitigating the ethical risks of AI products that are developed in-house and procured from third-party vendors. More specifically, when product and procurement teams bring a proposal for a solution to the AI Ethics Committee (hereafter AIEC), the responsibility of the committee is to:

1. Recommend against developing or procuring the solution
2. Confirm that that there are no ethical risks pertaining to the solution that would warrant the cessation of the development or procurement process
3. Recommend feature changes to the proposed solution that, if adopted, would lead to the second judgment in a further review.

This process lends itself to one that can itself be overseen and audited. That is because the AIEC should document all cases that come before it, which includes a record of its recommendations. As for how it comes to decide on one, two, or three, your AIEC should be guided by your AI ethics statement and your AI ethical case law. In fact, your AIEC may have as one of its responsibilities the creation of that ethical case law in the first place.

Creating an AIEC will require a host of decisions, none more important than who should serve on the committee and what its jurisdiction should be.

Membership

An AIEC requires a diverse team of experts. You'll want a data scientist who understands the technical underpinnings of the research or product so the committee can understand what is being done and what can be done from a technical perspective. Similarly, someone deeply familiar with product design is important. They speak the language of the product developers, understand customer journeys, and can help shape ethical risk-mitigation strategies in a way that doesn't undermine the essential functions of the products under consideration. You'll also want to include ethics-adjacent members, like attorneys and privacy officers. Their knowledge of current and potential regulations, antidiscrimination law, and privacy practices are important places to look when vetting for ethical risks.

Because the AIEC has as its function the identification and mitigation of *ethical* risks, you would be wise to include an ethicist, that is, someone with a PhD in philosophy who specializes in ethics or, say, someone with a master's degree in medical ethics. The ethicist isn't there to act as a kind of priest with superior ethical views. They're there because they have training, knowledge, and experience related to understanding and spotting a vast array of ethical risks, familiarity with important concepts and distinctions that aid in clear-eyed ethical deliberation, and the skill of helping groups of people objectively assess ethical issues. In fact, as you've been reading this book, you've been guided by a person with a PhD in philosophy (despite my mom preferring an MD) through the landscape of AI ethics, attempting to show you the kinds of risks, how they arise, some important distinctions to help you in your ethical deliberations, and so on.

Also include various subject-matter experts depending on the research or product. If the product is to be deployed in universities, someone deeply familiar with their operations, goals, and constituencies should be included. If the product is to be deployed in Japan, an expert in Japanese culture may be important.

Last, as part of an effort to maintain independence and the absence of conflict of interests (e.g., members looking for approval from their bosses), have at least one member unaffiliated with your organization (which is, incidentally, required for medical IRBs). At the same time, all members should have a sense of the business goals and necessities.

Jurisdiction

When should your product teams consult an AIEC and how much power should it have?

Even though AI ethical risks are realized during deployment, not research and product development, an AIEC should be consulted before research or product development begins. The primary rationale for this was revealed in each of the chapters on bias, explainability, and privacy, and made explicit in Structure from Content Lessons 3, 5, and 8. Another powerful reason that is more pragmatic is that it's much easier—and therefore more inexpensive and efficient—to change projects and products that do not yet exist. If, for instance, you only realize a significant ethical risk from a potential or probable unintended consequence of how the product was designed, you will either have to go to market with a product you know to be ethically risky or you will have to go through the costly process of reengineering the product.

Now comes especially consequential decisions. I can't stress their importance enough.

1. Are product development and procurement teams *required* to consult the AIEC or is it merely recommended?

2. Are the decisions of the AIEC *requirements* that product and procurement teams must follow or are they merely recommendations? And if they are required, can a senior executive nonetheless *overrule* them?

How serious are you, really, about identifying and mitigating ethical risks? Is it a nice-to-have or a need-to-have? How much do you care about protecting both people and your brand's reputation? These decisions reveal your answers. Let's look at the possibilities. (See table 6-1.)

In the table, the two black ovals indicate high risk. If consulting the AIEC is a mere recommendation, a (probably small) subset of your teams will use it. And only a subset of that subset will actually take its recommendations. The result is lots of risk still on the table. And in the very odd scenario in which you do not require teams to consult the AIEC, but their decisions are requirements, no one will consult it for fear of being objectionably constrained.

TABLE 6-1

Risks, authority, and your ethics committee

	AIEC decisions are requirements	AIEC decisions are recommendations
Consulting AIEC required	○ (Low risk)	● gray (Medium risk)
Consulting AIEC recommended	● black (High risk)	● black (High risk)

Table key

○ = Low risk

● gray = Medium risk

● black = High risk

Things are slightly better if everyone is required to consult the AIEC, but its decisions are recommendations. For some teams, learning about some risks they weren't previously aware of will provide sufficient motivation to make the appropriate changes to the product. But teams who are in love with their idea, or who think the AIEC is overreacting, or think all this ethics stuff is nonsense, will carry on as though they never consulted the AIEC. That's risky for them, of course, because they will be on record for willfully defying the recommendations of the AIEC, but there are lots of risk takers out there.

That said, it's a very serious thing to create an AIEC that product and procurement teams are required to consult and whose decisions are requirements. That's a lot of power, and it can have a real business impact. But there is at least one strong reason you should consider voluntarily granting that degree of power to your AIEC: it is a tool by which great trust is built with employees, clients, consumers, and other stakeholders, like government regulators. That is particularly true if your organization is transparent about the operations—even if not the exact decisions—of the committee. If being an ethically sound company is at the top of the pyramid of your company's values, then granting an AIEC the independence and power to veto proposals is a good idea.

Companies that are not ready to grant that kind of power to an internal committee but are also committed to AI ethical risk mitigation can find a kind of middle ground. They can allow the AIEC to be overruled by a senior executive, most likely someone in the C-suite. That would allow organizations to take ethical risks when they think it's *really* worth it, but for the default consisting in the AIEC being the final word.

All this is for those who are convinced an AIEC ought to be chosen. Those who think that it's not worth the trouble or it's not necessary to create one can expect problems to occur regularly, including courting many opportunities for conflicts of interest (e.g., between the short-term career goals of those developing or procuring products and the long-term welfare of the organization's brand), inconsistencies within and among different departments, and an increased probability of failure to identify AI ethical risks.

5. Accountability

It's imperative that you assign role-specific responsibilities aimed at identifying and mitigating AI ethical risks. This will include responsibilities for data collectors, data scientists and engineers, product owners, and more. And just as responsibilities assigned to a role in any other circumstance, failure to fulfill those responsibilities must be taken seriously. Product teams can easily discount the importance of faithfully and sincerely adhering to the processes required of them if flouting them has zero financial impact.

Ample empirical evidence indicates that organizations that turn a blind financial eye to ethical risks will realize those risks. Wells Fargo, for instance, infamously incentivized its employees to manufacture new accounts out of whole cloth; the incentive structure made that ethical lapse probable.[2] Further, if your product people who adhere to the ethical practices puts them at a competitive disadvantage for bonuses, raises, and promotions in comparison to their ethics-processes-flouting peers, they are likely to relax their own standards.

On the other hand, regularly recognizing, both informally (e.g., shout-outs at meetings) and formally (e.g., promotions), the sincere adoption and promotion of the AI ethical standards of your organization will vastly increase the probability of continued adoption and even improvement of the system, as eager employees see that improving the system is not just a reward unto itself.

Upholding the AI ethical standards articulated in your AI ethics statement and your ethical case law and made manifest in the tools you give your product teams and the processes by which they should develop, procure, and deploy AI must appear in quarterly or annual evaluations, informal encouragements, and ultimately, the way in which you financially compensate your team.

6. An AI Ethical Risk Program with KPIs

You need an AI ethical risk program that is created, scaled, and maintained in a measurable way. Your AIEC can take the lead on this with the oversight of a senior executive.

Distinguish between (1) the extent to which the organization is adopting or complying with these new standards and (2) the extent to which meeting those standards sufficiently mitigates risk. The first is of a piece with familiar risk and compliance programs. Your compliance teams can measure, for instance, what percent of product proposals your AIEC rejects or accepts, the average number of rounds of revisions in light of AIEC recommendations, the number of staff that have faced disciplinary action for flouting the AI ethics program, how widely and how well the standards are understood across the organization, and so on. If your policies are well written, they'll include an articulation of what successful implementation of the policies looks like and how to measure and track progress.

The second typically trips people up. They want to know if they're *actually* achieving their ethical goals or avoiding their ethical nightmares. "But what are KPIs for justice, respect, and privacy?" people routinely ask. Having no idea how to measure such things, they're stumped.

We've already seen why they're stumped: these terms are so abstract and high level that it's no wonder why you can't simply announce you're "for" them and then go on to measure them. On the other hand, if you have a substantive AI ethics statement and AI ethical case law, you've got some meat on the bones to measure.

If you've committed to never falling below level three of privacy as outlined in chapter 4, you can measure the percentage of products that fall below that level and track your progress over time. If you've committed to having all consumer-facing ML products that distribute a good or service explainable to your average consumer, that's something you can routinely test for and measure. If you want to ensure that your commitment to inclusion is manifested in how you approach ML bias mitigation, you can test the approval ratings of your chosen metrics with relevant stakeholders. And so on.

Your Structure will get clearer and easier to measure *if you take great care in determining and articulating your Content.* If your Content is vague and open-ended, you'll have a hard time keeping track of and measuring it. If your Content is detailed and illuminating, it's all downhill after that.

7. Executive Ownership

Creating an AI ethical risk program requires organizational and cultural change. If you're going to create an AIEC with teeth, if your product teams are going to use new tools and engage in new processes, if individuals and teams will be held accountable for complying with your AI ethical risk program, if training is to be taken seriously, if your teams will be evaluated, at least in part, by their performance as measured by various KPIs, then a senior executive, ideally in the C-suite, needs to own this. This cannot be a bottom-up approach. At most, the bottom can spearhead activities that prompt senior leadership to take it seriously, but the systematic and comprehensive adoption of AI ethical risk strategies comes from, and is sustained by, the top. Insofar as they are charged with protecting the long-term value of the organization, the board of directors of any organization that develops, procures, and deploys AI would be negligent in failing to ensure that a senior executive is leading the charge.

This might be obvious, but while it's obvious in principle, it is not always obvious in practice. The initial instinct I routinely push against with my clients is to give the reins of the AI ethics program to a senior person on the product team who is not in the C-suite. The thought is reasonable: "We don't want our AI products to be ethically risky, so let's make sure the product teams own this." And if it's not a senior product person, then it's a senior engineer. "Our head of product isn't an engineer or data scientist, and there's a lot of technical stuff here. Let's give this to the engineering leads."

The rationale behind these thoughts makes sense. "When AI products go ethically wrong, that's bad, and so we need people close to the product to take ownership." But those people—unless we're talking about the chief product officer or chief data, analytics, or AI officer—don't have the power to lead a program that pushes the kind of organizational change that an AI ethics program requires. They do not, for instance, have any sway in the marketing and HR departments that are procuring AI from vendors.

So, yes, in a way, the fact that executive ownership is needed is obvious. But that obvious fact tends to dim when operationalizing gets real; don't let it.

Recap

- AI ethical risks are many and varied. The big three challenges—bias, explainability, and privacy—loom large, but many ethical risks result from particular use cases. Senior leaders are responsible for creating, scaling, and maintaining an AI ethical risk program that comprehensively, systematically, and thoughtfully addresses these risks.
- Creating your organization's AI ethical case law is an extremely powerful tool in articulating the organization's AI ethical standards and communicating them to relevant stakeholders, including especially product developers and ethics committees.
- AI ethical risks are not just a product or techie problem. They're for anyone in the organization who procures and uses machine learning tools.
- It would be unwise and unfair to charge data scientists, engineers, and product developers or owners with the primary

responsibility of identifying and mitigating ethical risks of products. Expert oversight is needed, most obviously in the form of an AI ethics committee. The degree of power you choose to bestow upon your AIEC is an extremely consequential decision that sets the tone and effectiveness of your AI ethical risk program.

- All parties must be held accountable—provided with both incentives and disincentives—for complying with the AI ethical risk program.

- Risk and compliance teams are well versed in determining appropriate KPIs for compliance with policies and processes. But determining KPIs for your actual ethical performance—by the lights of your own ethical standards in conjunction with existing regulatory and legal standards—follows from the depth of the articulation of your AI ethical standards in your AI ethics statement and your AI ethical case law. The higher their quality, the higher quality your KPIs will be for your ethical performance.

- Excitement about AI ethics from junior people is a wonderful thing, but there is no such thing as a viable and robust AI ethical risk program without leadership and ownership from the top.

7

AI Ethics for Developers

The standard line in AI ethics is that product teams—including product managers or owners, data scientists, engineers, and designers—need "tools" to think about the ethical risks of their products. (I put the word "tools" in scare quotes because it's a term that gets thrown around all the time and encompasses so many kinds of things—from lists of questions with qualitative answers to quantitative or mathematical analyses to lists of alleged ethical best practices—that it's nearly meaningless.) This is a reasonable thought and, on the whole, it's true. But divorced from a larger context, it's also misleading.

If teams aren't interested in using the tools (you don't have their buy-in), the tools don't fit their workflow (they're not embedded in the process in the right way or the tools haven't been customized to fit their needs), or there's no organizational incentive to use the tools (there are no role-specific responsibilities with regard to who uses the tools, there's no accountability), then you can throw all the tools you like at your teams and it won't make a bit of difference.

In other words, ignore the conclusions of the last chapter and tools can't save you.

What's more, it assumes that these tools are effective at creating a team that can do the job required of them. This is like giving me a chainsaw and a hammer and nails and telling me to build a house; it's not gonna be pretty. It won't even be functional. Tools are efficiently and effectively wielded when their users are equipped with the requisite concepts, knowledge, and training. This chapter provides that requisite background. And it's important not only for those on the ground developing, but also for those overseeing the teams, including an AIEC and senior executives.

First, Three Ways to Shift a Product Team's Focus

We're going to start by slightly shifting your focus. My experience working with companies shows me there's three areas where they don't get it quite right. A slight adjustment will improve the odds of success when implementing an AI ethics program.

First, product teams—the ones that say they do "ethics by design"—often think they should view AI ethics through the "lenses" of moral theories found in philosophy. This reflects a blinkered view of what ethical analysis consists of. Instead, companies can and should think about this topic far more practically and rigorously.

Second, product teams, if they think about ethics, primarily think in terms of avoiding harming people. I would reframe this to stress the importance of *not wronging people.*

Third, companies pretend, or actually believe, that there are no such things as ethicists, or that they are merely academic creatures with no real-world experience. This is wrong. Expertise matters.

We'll take each of these in turn.

1. Don't appeal to ethical theories

I frequently hear it suggested that AI developers should consider various ethical or moral theories to aid them in ethical risk identification: "Let's consider this through the lens of utilitarianism." "Consider a Kantian perspective." Or WWAD: "What would Aristotle do?"

This is a terrible way to build ethically sound AI.

When people think about moral theories, they're usually thinking about three schools of (academic) ethics that mean to tell us, roughly, which things are good or bad, right or wrong, and why. Briefly the three schools are:

Consequentialism—of which utilitarianism is one example—which says the right thing to do is whatever brings about the best consequences overall.

Deontology—of which Immanuel Kant's theory is an example—which says an act is right or wrong independently of its consequences. Rather, it's right or wrong depending on its conformity (or lack thereof) to a set of principles; you break the rules, you did something wrong, even if everything turned out all right.

Virtue ethics—of which Aristotle's view is an example—which says the right thing to do is that which the virtuous person does. Would the courageous (or generous, or kind, etc.) person do it? If yes, it's the right thing to do. If not, it's the wrong thing to do.

These theories have impressive and influential intellectual pedigrees. Almost any professor of philosophy who works on ethics knows them in more than a little detail. But again, turning to them to help with your products is a terrible idea.

First, these things aren't "perspectives" or "lenses." They are incompatible moral theories. If you think an act is right by virtue of the consequences it brings about, you're not a deontologist. If you think an act can be right independently of its consequences, you're not a utilitarian. Thus, the idea that you take your ethical problem, sprinkle some utilitarianism and Kantianism on it (perhaps with a pinch of virtue ethics), and come to a well-formed conclusion is fundamentally misguided.

Second, different people on a given team will have different views on which moral theory is the most plausible (and many people on the team won't be able to muster enough motivation to even begin to form an opinion). Given that you're trying to make progress in identifying ethical risks so you can make progress in product development, pausing to engage in discussions about moral theories is a (fascinating, in my view, but I admit not terribly valuable in this context) distraction.

Third, even if you did pause to discuss the plausibility of these theories and everyone agreed that, say, utilitarianism is the coolest kid on the block, now you'll have to decide which of the dozens of incompatible varieties of utilitarianism you should go with.

Fourth, these theories are meant to explain which things are right or wrong and why. They are not, at least primarily, intended to be used as decision-making procedures. Newtonian physics is a true theory of how medium-sized objects operate on earth, but you would not be well advised to consult its axioms while playing baseball.

Fifth, in identifying ethical risks in product development, you're looking for places where you agree that something is risky. You don't need to agree on the theory that explains why this is ethically risky. For instance, both you and your colleague can think systematically discriminating against people of color in hiring is wrong. One of you may think this for broadly utilitarian reasons, while the other thinks this broadly for deontological reasons. But who cares? What matters for the case at hand is that you both think this is an ethical risk that needs to be mitigated and then you can get to work collaboratively identifying and executing on risk-mitigation strategies.

Sixth, moral theories can easily serve to rationalize ethical conclusions that people have already come to. The theories can be used to serve people's agendas, rather than informing what those agendas ought to be.

Seventh, work by ethicists in which concrete cases are discussed—for instance, in the medical ethics literature that has informed laws, regulations, and policies—never proceeds by way of a ham-handed "application" of a moral theory. Ethical reasoning, like legal reasoning, is far more subtle than that, and often proceeds by way of analogical reasoning, as we saw in our discussion of ethical case law.

2. Focus on wrongs

Another approach to ethical risk analysis among product teams is to talk about "harm." "We must ensure that we don't harm people," "We should consider the stakeholders that might be harmed," and "Consider the ways people might be harmed by this product." This is a reasonable thought. But thinking primarily in terms of harm and its contrary, benefit, invites a certain way of thinking that's not always helpful in the context of ethical risk identification.

There's a difference between harming someone and wronging them, and we can see this in two ways: we can wrong people without harming them and we can harm them without wronging them.

You can wrong someone in a variety of ways, including (but not limited to) breaking a promise you made to them, denying them access to various goods and services to which they have a right, failing to repay a debt to them, failing to help them when they are in dire need and it costs you little to nothing to save them, denying them due process in a legal context, and physically assaulting them.

You could protest that all these are ways of harming people, but that would only muddy the conceptual and thus deliberative waters. Perhaps I broke a promise I made to you, but you don't care; you never wanted that thing I promised to you anyway. Or I fail to repay a loan to you, but you're so wealthy now you won't feel the difference whether I repay you or not. Maybe I deny you a promotion that you deserve, but you were going to quit whether you received it or not. Or maybe you get denied a job on the grounds that you're Black or a woman, but had you not been discriminated against, you still wouldn't have gotten the job because you lack the requisite training or experience; you've been wronged, even if not having been wronged would have landed you in exactly the same place (viz. unemployed). All of this is to say that we can wrong people without harming them.

Going the other way now, we can harm people without wronging them. For instance, you may harm someone in self-defense or in order to protect someone else. Those are not cases in which you've wronged someone; you can be justified in your harmful actions. That said, harming someone or something (e.g., a group of people) is, on the face of it, wrong, and so those actions do deserve extra attention by asking, "Is it justifiable to produce this harm in this case?"

It's also easy to confuse harming someone with having a negative impact on them. For instance, you may have gotten a promotion over someone and so you've negatively impacted them (by virtue of your superior performance, say), but you certainly haven't wronged them.

The same goes for products. For example, suppose you advise individual investors on how to allocate their money. Further, assume that your services are marketed in a way that any reasonable diversity and inclusion officer would condone. However, for a variety of reasons outside the control of your organization, one particular subpopulation uses your services more than others. If your clients now acquire wealth and capital, you've created a differential impact between the subpopulation that uses your services and those that do not. But you have not wronged the latter subpopulations, even if they are now, all else equal, worse off than your clients.

You may nonetheless find this result unacceptable, and as a result, you may put more effort into marketing and selling to those subpopulations. Indeed, it may be that your AI ethics statement commits you to doing more. But while that is ethically good and even admirable, failing to do so is not equivalent to harming, let alone wronging, those subpopulations. If your AI ethics commitments include, say, driving toward equity in everything you do, it will not only lead you to not harming or wronging people, but also to going above and beyond the call of duty.

Perhaps most importantly, the idea that you should not harm people can come into conflict with other ethical imperatives, for example, that you should respect people's autonomy. Selling cigarettes to you may result in your net harm, but it would be objectionably paternalistic of me to refuse to sell them to you. That's because respecting your autonomy means respecting your decisions and your ability to act on them without interference from third parties (provided that you're not, for instance, breaking the law and I'm not manipulating you into buying them). A narrow focus on harms in ethical risk identification can thus blind one to other ethical risks.

This is exactly the kind of problem my client faced. They use AI to make recommendations regarding what kind of ad content to consume. The company thought, not unreasonably, "We are committed to the well-being of our audience, and that means we need to recommend a certain kind of content over others, for instance, content that inspires and informs instead of content that provides meaningless ephemeral pleasures." Admirable as its commitment to user well-being is, it may nonetheless infringe on its users' individual autonomy as you provide them with content you think is good for them instead of what they think is good for them, which would entail giving users more control over the kind of content they are recommended. In fact, this very point was made by one of the company's primary partners. The result was figuring out how, exactly, to design the product and articulate ethical best practices for its deployment in a way that sufficiently respects people's autonomy. That satisfied the partner and the company's own commitment to not wronging its audience.

Last—and this comes from years of teaching thousands of students—when people think about harming someone, they often focus on the harmed people's psychological states, for instance, whether the person feels (physical or emotional) pain. When we think about wronging people, on the other hand, people focus more on whether we are either defaulting on our own obligations to them or violating their rights or otherwise stopping them from receiving something they deserve. Those are two very different places to start thinking about an ethical issue.

For example, if you're focused on harm, you might think about the men who are extremely psychologically distraught that you're giving tools to women by which they can educate themselves and make themselves more independent. You're harming those men. But is this harm morally relevant? Should it guide our decisions? Should we balance their harm against the harm done to the women? (And it's even more complicated if the women prefer to be treated that way.) Do we settle this question by taking a survey to see how many people are pained by this and how many people are pleased by it? I doubt it.

On the other hand, if you ask whether you're wronging anyone, the focus is on her rights (and his, if there are any in this context) and our own obligations when we enter the situation. Harming him by causing him psychological distress isn't an area of moral focus because we don't automatically assume that harming someone is always bad.

In light of these issues with a "stakeholder harm" approach, I recommend thinking in terms of wronging people, what's ethically permissible, what rights might be violated, and what obligations might be defaulted on.

This is not to say that talking about harming people isn't legitimate. It's to say that it should not take center stage. In fact, it did not take center stage in the chapters on bias, explainability, and privacy. Unequal distributions of goods and services across various subpopulations are wrong in some cases but not in others (even if those latter cases differentially benefit some subpopulations and thereby disadvantage others). Failing to provide someone with an explanation may be a failure to express a level of respect that person is owed, and they are thus wronged in not receiving that explanation. Collecting data about a person when they explicitly and not unreasonably demand that the data not be collected is a way of wronging someone even if it doesn't actually result in harm. And finally, violating your commitments as laid out in your AI ethics statement would be wrong even if it doesn't result in harming anyone; you made a promise, after all.

3. Get ethicists involved

I've been at pains to stress that expert oversight is needed, and more specifically, ethicists are needed. In the last chapter I recommended that an ethicist be a member of your AI Ethics Committee. I also recommend incorporating them during product design, for three reasons.

One, ethicists are able to spot ethical problems much faster than designers, engineers, and data scientists (just as the latter can spot bad design, faulty engineering, and flawed mathematical analyses, respectively, much faster than ethicists). Given that your organization likely wants to scale ethical risk identification without slamming on the brakes of product development, speed to identification is an important factor.

Two, various projects give rise to a host of ethical questions, and it's easy to get lost when trying to answer them. Ethicists have the conceptual repertoire, experience, and skill set needed to navigate these issues and to help others navigate them as well (as I've tried to do in the above discussion on harming versus wronging). A comparison with legal risks is instructive. Not only will the lawyer be faster at spotting legal risks, but she will also be better at thinking through them and in helping others think through them. Teams do not need ethicists working with them full-time, but rather as subject-matter experts that are consulted when appropriate. These ethicists can be procured on an as-needed basis or, depending on the size of the organization and the quantity and speed at which products are developed, internal ethicists that float among a variety of teams.

Three, human-centric design has led many product developers to consult relevant stakeholders throughout the design process. Similarly, some people have suggested that AI developers engage in "value-sensitive design" in which products are made in light of the values of the people who will be affected directly or indirectly by deployment of the product. These recommendations are reasonable. But people can value things that, when acted on, violate people's rights or harm them in some other way. Think about, for instance, men who value women being in subordinate social roles that forbid them from voting or receiving a legitimate education. What should a value-sensitive designer do in this instance? Respect the valuers? Respect an ethical standard that those stakeholders explicitly deny? What should guide that decision? Navigating these kinds of conflicts and helping others to find their way is one place where ethicists have a wealth of training and experience, making for a relatively speedy and robust due diligence process.

Can We Talk about Tools Now?

Not quite yet. We need an understanding of what the team needs to think about, and in some cases, it extends beyond the product team. More specifically, there are five issues to focus on with regard to ethical risk identification in the products you're developing, procuring, and deploying.

1. What you create
2. How you create it
3. What people do with it
4. What impacts it has
5. What you do about those impacts

In each of these categories, there are questions to ask pertaining to the identification and mitigation of ethical risks. To focus our questions, consider the following real-life case.

The British police force decided to use facial-recognition software along with its vast network of closed-circuit television (CCTV) cameras. The facial-recognition technology turned out to be biased against people of color, falsely identifying them as suspects at higher rates than white people. This, in turn, led to harassing perfectly innocent people whose faces were mistakenly identified as that of someone in the police database. It also led to nonprofit organizations suing the police force, not to mention being featured in a very unfavorable light in the widely distributed and viewed documentary, *Coded Bias.*

What was created? A product that married facial-recognition technology with a list of suspects that could interface with CCTV footage. *How did they create it?* In part, by using data that resulted in discriminatory outputs. *What did people do with it?* The police used it to detain, question, and in some cases, harass innocent citizens (including a fourteen-year-old Black boy, as depicted in the documentary). *What impacts did it have?* Violating people's privacy, a lawsuit, unfavorable news coverage, sowing distrust of the police. *What did they do about the impacts?* Among other things, they're spending time and resources defending against the lawsuit.

For each product your team is working on, there are questions pertaining to the ethical risks of each of the five categories listed. Answering these questions is part of an overall due diligence process. More specifically, that due diligence requires answering five questions.

1. What are the ethical risks involved in what we are proposing to create (or procure)?

In the case of the police surveillance technology, putting the issue of discrimination aside, one can already see the potential for privacy violations. After all, this is a technology that, when it does what it's supposed to do, tracks individuals' movements throughout a city: where they go, who they go there with, how they get there, and so on. Further, since police forces are present where the technology is being deployed, it lends itself to continual police interference with one's life. A question immediately presents itself to the team responsible for bringing the product to the police force: Should we do this, or does it threaten to violate people's privacy to too great an extent? And then, if it's decided it will be used, how can we develop and deploy this product in a way that mitigates the risk of violations of privacy? Perhaps the answer here could involve the video only being used after the fact instead of live, or that it can only be used when searching for a particular individual for whom there is sufficient evidence that they are worth investigating for a crime as determined by a judge (in the way that search warrants need to be approved by a judge). Or perhaps it can only be used for a certain level of crime, or when the supposed criminal plausibly presents an imminent threat, or when the probability of being accurate crosses a certain threshold, and so on.

What ethical risks might we realize by virtue of how we create the product?

Here the issue is whether the way in which it is created gives rise to ethical risk. For instance, could the product we're making possibly offer biased or discriminatory outputs? What might some data sets look like that would plausibly result in discriminatory outputs? Is this a case in which we need explainable outputs? If so, how important is explainability in this context relative to accuracy? Who do we need to provide explanations to and what will they need to be able to do with those explanations? Are we potentially making predictions about people in a way that could violate their privacy? And so on.

In the case of the facial-recognition product used by the British police, not only were they using a privacy-invading technology by virtue of the particular use case for this AI, but they were also using a discriminatory model. (This has led some people to decry the existence of biased facial-recognition technology. This is, in some cases, a bit odd. If being surveilled is bad, you probably want the product to be really bad at its job. Protesting that a company's privacy-invading surveillance software doesn't recognize the faces of people of color is a bit like the old Woody Allen facetious restaurant review: the food is terrible, and the portions are too small.)

How might people use the product in a way that is ethically risky?

You might build a car with cutting-edge safety features, but how people operate that car can still be dangerous. There are well-intentioned but ignorant or not-too-sharp operators, reckless drivers (from drunk driving to texting while driving to teenagers just "having some fun"), and positively bad-intentioned people who are looking to hurt someone. In other words, deployment matters.

In the case of British police, while it's easy to imagine some very smart and well-trained officers using the product wisely, it is equally easy to imagine under-trained and under-brained officers making bad judgments about how to use it. It's also easy to imagine the bad-apple cop who abuses it to suit his own ends. When creating or procuring AI, due diligence needs to be done here as well. Product teams need to think about the diverse array of people who might use their product and what ethical risks could result from what ignorant, dumb, and malicious users might do with it. In light of those findings, product teams need to think about what features to (not) include in the product to mitigate those risks. Further, because safety features can only go so far, those teams also need to articulate ethical best practices for use of the product and ensure that information is communicated clearly to users of the product. For instance, if your team is building an AI that your clients will use, an organization can include in its onboarding process a clear articulation of the ethical risk due diligence your product team (and, ideally, your AIEC) performed and the ethical best practices for use of the product.

What ethical risks, some of which have been realized, result from deploying this product?

This is outside the product team's scope, but it's important to highlight when talking about the ethical risks of particular products. Notice that the question presupposes that the organization is monitoring the impacts of the product through, for instance, surveys, stakeholder interviews, and various technical ways to measure the data that's collected by the product (including, for instance, measuring whether the data you're getting back, which you'll use to continue to train your AI, might cause or exacerbate discriminatory outputs).

AI products are a bit like circus tigers. You raise them like they're your own, you train them carefully, they perform beautifully in show after show after show, and then one day they bite your head off. For tigers, that's roughly because of their natures. For AI, it's more the result of nurture: how we trained it, how it behaves in the wild, how we continue to train it with more data, and how it interacts with the various environments it's embedded in. Data scientists already monitor their deployed AI for things like data drift: the new data that is inputted is sufficiently different from the data you originally trained your AI with that now the model isn't working as you'd like. This happened with many models as a result of the Covid-19 pandemic: suddenly March 2020 data looked a lot different from February 2020 data, not to mention March 2019 data. The result was some really bad predictions by AI models that were meant to tell users what March 2020 should look like (e.g., financial market predictions). Similarly, because of more variables than one can count—changing demographics of a city, uneven adoption by different ages, races, genders, new laws and regulations, evolving cultural norms, to name a few—one's AI can be ethically riskier than it was on the day you deployed it.

What do you do about the ethical risks spotted after deployment?

Once those ethical risks are spotted, we have to start back with our first question. Given what things are like now, what are the ethical risks of our product, and do we need to pull the product or are there ways we can modify it to sufficiently mitigate those ethical risks? How do we continue to create this product in a way that mitigates the risks we didn't foresee but have not materialized or look like they might? What kinds of people are using our product in ways we didn't foresee that we now need to account for? In other words, ethical risk identification and mitigation is not something product teams are ever finished and done with, or at least, they're not finished and done until the life cycle of the product is finished and done.

We've just covered a lot of ground so let's summarize as succinctly as possible:

> We need to identify how we might wrong people by virtue of what we're creating, how we're creating it, who's using it, and what unforeseen impacts it has.

From this, two questions present themselves:

1. When do we engage in these investigations?

2. How do we engage in them?

And now, at last, we've come to processes and tools.

Processes and Tools: When and How

It is always easier and cheaper to alter a fictional product than an already existing one that people have poured time and resources into. For that reason, the first three questions—what are the ethical risks of the product we're proposing to create, how might we create it an ethically risky way, and what ethical risks may arise with different kinds of users—are appropriate when brainstorming what the product or "solution" might be. It also makes sense to incorporate these issues during product road-map planning and feature creation.

At this early stage, various proposals might be rejected because they are clearly too high an ethical risk, other proposals may get extra points because they're apparently low risk, and other proposals will be modified in light of the identification of ethical risks.

There are various tools one might use at this stage to structure the ethical risk due diligence the team is performing. While those tools vary and I won't provide a review of any particular tool here, the tool your teams choose should include at least the following.

First, a breakdown of ethical risk by categories. Different tools slice the pie differently, and in my work, I use the following categories:

- Physical harm (e.g., death, injury)
- Mental harm (e.g., addiction, anxiety, depression)
- Autonomy (e.g., violations of privacy)
- Trustworthiness and respect (e.g., failing to provide necessary explanations; taking the well-being of users, consumers, or citizens seriously)

- Relationships and social cohesion (e.g., sowing social distrust, polarizing populations)
- Social justice and fairness (e.g., discriminatory outputs, violating human rights, wealth inequality)
- Unintended consequences (e.g., unintended consequences arising from both true positives or negatives and false positives or negatives, use by ignorant, dumb, or malicious people)

Notice that, unlike many other frameworks for identifying ethical risks, I have not made "discriminatory outputs" its own category, despite the importance of the issue. That is because, while discriminatory models are an affront to justice and fairness, there are other ways of violating the requirements of justice. Taking a larger view of justice that includes but is not limited to the issue of discrimination is essential to ensure the comprehensiveness of your due diligence. Similarly, while explainability may be ethically important—because it may be required for being trustworthy and respectful of the people on whom you deploy your AI—failing to provide an explanation is not the only way you can violate trust and respect. Here, too, comprehensiveness requires that we consider the broader category, even if certain members of that category should be flagged as deserving particular attention.

Second, an articulation of the various stakeholders, for example, users of the AI, those about whom the AI makes predictions, communities or subpopulations that might be impacted by wide-scale deployment of the AI, and so on.

Third, an assessment of how those various stakeholders may be wronged by your product in each of those categories.

TABLE 7-1

Ethical risk due diligence framework

	Physical harm	Mental harm	Autonomy	Trust & respect	Relationships & social cohesion	Social justice & fairness	Unintended consequences
Stakeholder A (for instance, a set of individuals)	●	◍	◍	○	●	○	●
Stakeholder B (a collective, for instance, a country, a community)	◍	●	◍	●	●	○	○
Stakeholder C	●	○	●	○	○	◍	●
Stakeholder D	○	○	◍	○	●	◍	○

Table key

○ = Low risk

◍ = Medium risk

● = High risk

Fourth, a way of prioritizing those risks in light of the probability of those wrongs being perpetrated and the degree of wrongness involved. (We don't usually talk about degrees of wrongness, but while unprovoked murder and unprovoked pushing are both wrong, the former is clearly more wrong than the latter.)

Putting all these together, your tool should look something like that in table 7-1.

You can use this same chart when assessing actual impacts of deployment of the product. This chart can only be filled out, of course, as a consequence of your team's investigation into the ethical risks. As for how to conduct that inquiry, once again, tools vary. They might include, among other things, a list of questions for each category (akin to a checklist); how your AI ethics statement and your AI ethical case law might bear on the issue; thinking about which of the five ethical levels of privacy you want to achieve; using a decision tree to determine whether explainability is important; engaging in premortem analysis (where you imagine things have gone wrong and work backward to figure out how things might have turned out that way). They might also include conducting stakeholder interviews, surveys, or analyses; ethical red teaming (where people try to ethically break the product); playing devil's advocate (where people argue for making the product ethically terrible); playing angel's advocate (where people argue for making the product as ethically good as possible); and as I have mentioned before, consulting an ethicist or having an ethicist facilitate the discussion.

But beware! When your team first gathers to talk about these issues, someone's going to start banging on about the subjectivity of ethics, and it's going to stymie the investigation. Tell them to read chapter 1. Or better yet, kick off this new practice with a discussion of chapter 1 and bake it into onboarding new members of the team.

Last, you'll then have to think about the big and small changes to the product that will change the black and gray to white.

In some cases, the due diligence will lead teams to realize they may need to reach outside their immediate team to mitigate an identified ethical risk. For instance, if model developers are part of the due diligence process and data collectors are not, and discriminatory output is identified as an ethical risk of the product, the former will have to discuss with the latter what they need the (training) data set to look like or, put differently, what it can't look like. On the other side of things—that is, after the model is deployed—data collectors will have to proactively monitor the data the AI software is bringing in and potentially retraining on. That information must then be relayed to the team developing the product so that it can properly reassess the ethical risks and create and execute on a risk-mitigation strategy, for example, devising different methods of collecting data, augmenting the data with synthetic data, modifying the new data, and so on.

Tools and processes are important. But they only make sense when embedded in a larger framework of what a product team is trying to accomplish. In this case, product teams are trying to avoid wronging people by virtue of what the team is creating, how it creates it, and who might get their hands on the product, where the conception of what wrongs are particularly important to avoid are informed by an AI ethics statement and an organization's AI ethics case law. Further, those tools that are meant to achieve those goals only work if they are nestled inside a larger organizational framework of the kind articulated in the previous chapter. Approaching AI ethical risk mitigation with the idea that we need to begin by providing our developers with tools is like starting a race at the finish line.

Recap

- AI ethical risk mitigation as it relates to product teams often focuses on moral theories, like consequentialism, deontology, and virtue ethics. Talking about or applying these theories should be dropped from the conversation.
- There is currently a massive focus on the avoidance of "harming" people. People would do well to focus on avoiding wronging people, where harming is just one way of wronging them.
- There is such a thing as ethical expertise. Those with that expertise are called "ethicists." Involve them.
- There are five issues to focus on with regards to ethical risk identification in the products you're developing, procuring, and deploying. Each of these issues relates to a question pertaining to ethical risk.

  1. What you create
     - *What are the ethical risks involved in what you are proposing to create or procure?*
  2. How you create it
     - *What are the ethical risks you might realize by virtue of how you create it?*
  3. What people do with it
     - *How might people use this in a way that is ethically risky?*

4. What impacts it has

    - *What are the ethical risks, some of which have been realized, as a result of deploying this product?*

5. What you do about those impacts

    - *What do you do about the ethical risks spotted after deployment?*

- Your team will have to engage in an ethical-risk due diligence process. At a minimum, that process should include:

    – A breakdown of ethical risks by category, where those categories exhaust the set of all possible ethical risks

    – An articulation of the various stakeholders

    – An assessment of how those stakeholders may be wronged by your product in each of the categories

    – A way of prioritizing risk mitigation in light of the probability of those stakeholders being wronged and the degree of wrongness involved

    – A way of determining what risk-mitigation strategies should be executed on, when, and by whom

CONCLUSION

Two Surprises

If you told me you were going to a conference on AI ethics, and that at a cocktail reception, you walked up to a group of attendees already discussing the topic, I could confidently tell you what was about to happen.

First, you're going to hear a lot of familiar phrases and buzzwords. You'll hear Accountability. Transparency. Explainability. Fairness. Surveillance. Governance. Trustworthy. Responsible. Stakeholders. Framework. Someone's going to say "black box" at some point.

Then, there'll be hand-wringing over the threats posed by AI gone wild. Biased data sets! Unexplainable algorithms! Invasions of privacy! Self-driving cars killing people!

Finally, the group will land on a healthy skepticism. "You can't really define AI ethics," you might hear. And "You can't plan for everything." Of course, also, "It's just people's own personal view of what's right and wrong." Or, more practically, "Look, how do you even operationalize ethical principles?" One person is going to say something about KPIs.

At the end of all this, there will be shrugs. That's because, for the most part, people are raising issues, the underpinnings of which are not (well) understood, and then, after they've put together a conference in which they sling buzzwords back and forth at each other, they declare AI ethics essential, of course, but also really, really difficult.

But not you. Having gotten to this point in the book, you can see those underpinnings. You see what's at issue, from both a business and an ethical perspective. And now that you understand it, you understand that AI ethics isn't so difficult after all.

If a colleague tells you, "We need to say something about AI ethics," you know what a meaningful document looks like and what's superficial PR.

If your colleague tells you, "This AI ethics is for the AI folks. It's technical. Tell them to get on it," you know how impoverished an understanding that is.

Maybe a company comes to you and says, "We have your solution for responsible AI" or, less ambitiously, "We have your solution for bias in AI." That piece of software, you now see, can't solve all those problems by itself.

You know that and so much more about, for example, the role of people in creating appropriate metrics for fairness. And about when you need to know what the AIs are doing and when it doesn't matter so much. You know there are levels of privacy, and it's not just about anonymity. You know how to build real AI ethics statements, and that just saying you value AI ethics doesn't mean your employees will take AI ethics seriously. You know you need Structure to make that happen. Most of all, you know software alone can neither handle the substantive ethical issues nor effect the kind of organizational change you need to systematically and comprehensively identify and mitigate AI's ethical risks. In short, provided the software can do its job, you see the ecosystem in which the software needs to get embedded.

You see the AI ethics landscape. Now, you can navigate it.

And now that you're here, I'm going to let you in on a secret. Two, actually.

The first secret is that there's another book in this book. Pretend chapters 1 and 5 through 7 are a single book and delete the word "AI" whenever I said "AI ethics." What you'll get, with some minor tweaks here and there, is a book on how to articulate and operationalize the ethical values of your organization. I don't care if you're developing AI, putting microchips in peoples' hands, or just selling bottled coffee: the way to create, scale, and maintain an ethically sound organization is already contained in those pages. If your aim is not only to create ethically sound AI, but to create an organization that takes ethical standards seriously, go back and reread those chapters with that in mind.

The second secret is that this book is about AI ethics, but it's not only about AI ethics. It's about the value of ethical inquiry. It's about the power and importance of philosophical investigation.

The many exercises you've gone through to understand AI ethics—pulling apart Structure from Content; distinguishing instrumental from noninstrumental values and ethical from nonethical values; understanding the differences between harming and wronging; distinguishing machine explanations from people explanations and assessing when and why each is important; critically examining the idea that ethics is subjective; analyzing what constitutes a good explanation; identifying the ethical levels of privacy and which levels are appropriate and when; drawing out the tensions between benevolence and respect for autonomy; breaking down the ethically salient questions in product development—*all* of this is philosophy in action. If you've found these distinctions, concepts, and analyses helpful in shedding light on the AI landscape, a landscape you didn't quite grasp before, then you've found philosophical analysis helpful. In understanding, internalizing, and thinking with these concepts, you're doing philosophy.

The main contention of this book is philosophical in nature. Structure—what to do and how to do it—flows from an understanding of Content, of the ethical risks and how they arise. Ethics looks squishy and subjective, and it's utterly unclear how to avoid disaster, until you dig deep to understand Content. It's not enough to understand AI. It's not even enough to understand risk and compliance. Engaging in robust and effective AI ethical risk mitigation requires understanding ethics at a level that goes well beyond "bias is bad" or "black boxes are scary."

Despite eye rolls and claims of irrelevance, philosophy turns out to be essential for the kind of progress we all ought to value.

NOTES

Introduction

1. Phil McCausland, "Self-driving Uber car that hit and killed woman did not recognize that pedestrians jaywalk," NBC News, November 9, 2019, https://www.nbcnews.com/tech/tech-news/self-driving-uber-car-hit-killed-woman-did-not-recognize-n1079281.

2. Melanie Evans and Anna Wilde Mathews, "New York Regulator Probes UnitedHealth Algorithm for Racial Bias," *Wall Street Journal*, October 26, 2019, https://www.wsj.com/articles/new-york-regulator-probes-unitedhealth-algorithm-for-racial-bias-11572087601.

3. Jeffrey Dastin, "Amazon scraps secret AI recruiting tool that showed bias against women," Reuters, October 10, 2018, https://www.reuters.com/article/us-amazon-com-jobs-automation-insight/amazon-scraps-secret-ai-recruiting-tool-that-showed-bias-against-women-idUSKCN1MK08G.

4. Kate Conger, Richard Fausset, and Serge F. Kovaleski, "San Francisco Bans Facial Recognition Technology," *New York Times*, May 14, 2019, https://www.nytimes.com/2019/05/14/us/facial-recognition-ban-san-francisco.html.

5. Julia Angwin et al., "Machine Bias," *ProPublica*, May 23, 2016, https://www.propublica.org/article/machine-bias-risk-assessments-in-criminal-sentencing.

6. "2020 in Review: 10 AI Failures," *Synced*, January 1, 2021, https://syncedreview.com/2021/01/01/2020-in-review-10-ai-failures/.

Chapter 2

1. Julia Angwin et al., "Machine Bias," *ProPublica*, May 23, 2016, https://www.propublica.org/article/machine-bias-risk-assessments-in-criminal-sentencing.

2. Alexandra Chouldechova, "Fair Prediction with Disparate Impact: A Study of Bias in Recidivism Prediction Instruments," paper, Cornell University, February 28, 2017, https://arxiv.org/abs/1703.00056.

3. This Structure from Content Lesson is about choosing the appropriate metric for fairness. "Appropriate" here means not only that different metrics for fairness are appropriate for different use cases, but also that different fairness metrics will alter the accuracy of your AI in different ways. As a result, the pitfalls of the various ways the tradeoffs can go should play a role in the decision about what fairness metric to use. The way in which fairness considerations can come into conflict with a demand for the most accurate AI is wonderfully presented in

Michael Kearns and Aaron Roth, the *Ethical Algorithm* (New York: Oxford University Press, 2020), chapter 2.

4. Joy Buolamwini and Timnit Gebru, "Gender Shades: Intersectional Accuracy Disparities in Commercial Gender Classification," Proceedings of the 1st Conference on Fairness, Accountability and Transparency, 2018, http://proceedings.mlr.press/v81/buolamwini18a.html.

5. Tom Simonite, "When It Comes to Gorillas, Google Photos Remains Blind," *Wired*, January 11, 2018, https://www.wired.com/story/when-it-comes-to-gorillas-google-photos-remains-blind/.

6. Alice Xiange, "Reconciling Legal and Technical Approaches to Algorithmic Bias," *Tennessee Law Review* 88, no. 3 (2021), https://ssrn.com/abstract=3650635.

7. If you're a data scientist, you might want to yell at me for always talking about accuracy and not precision or recall, let alone their harmonic mean. I hear you. These are important things to discuss when we get into the details of assessing particular models, and they bear on the potential ethical implications of the model. But alas, my audience is more general for this book, and so you and I will just have to discuss these things over coffee.

8. Bo Cowgill et al., "Biased Programmers? Or Biased Data? A Field Experiment in Operationalizing AI Ethics," research paper, Columbia Business School, June 24, 2020, https://papers.ssrn.com/sol3/papers.cfm?abstract_id=3615404.

Chapter 3

1. The issue here is the tension between explainability, on the one hand, and accuracy, on the other. See Chapter 2, endnote 3 for a bit about the tension between fairness and accuracy.

2. This famously happened with DeepMind's artificial intelligence software, AlphaGo, when it played the game of Go against Lee Sedol, a world-renowned player. It made a move—move 37—that was completely unexpected by all Go experts, but it was a stroke of "genius." https://www.wired.com/2016/03/two-moves-alphago-lee-sedol-redefined-future/.

Chapter 4

1. Todd Feathers, "Tech Companies Are Training AI to Read Your Lips," Vice, June 14, 2021, https://www.vice.com/en/article/bvzvdw/tech-companies-are-training-ai-to-read-your-lips.

Interlude

1. Many thanks to Philip Walsh, a fellow philosopher, who forced me to think about this issue more seriously when my initial instinct was to scoff. You win this round, Phil.

Chapter 5

1. "Seven Principles for AI: BMW Group Sets Out Code of Ethics for the Use of Artificial Intelligence," BMW Group, press release, December 10, 2020, https://www.press.bmwgroup.com/global/article/detail/T0318411EN/seven-principles-for-ai:-bmw-group-sets-out-code-of-ethics-for-the-use-of-artificial-intelligence?language=en.

2. "Guidelines for Artificial Intelligence," Deutsche Telekom, n.d., https://www.telekom.com/en/company/digital-responsibility/details/artificial-intelligence-ai-guideline-524366.

3. Corinna Machmeier, "SAP's Guiding Principles for Artificial Intelligence," SAP, September 18, 2018, https://news.sap.com/2018/09/sap-guiding-principles-for-artificial-intelligence/.

4. Ibid.

5. "Artificial Intelligence at Google, Our Principles," Google AI, n.d., https://ai.google/principles/.

6. The example comes from David Hume's famous discussion in Appendix I: Concerning Moral Sentiment in his *An Enquiry Concerning the Principles of Morals.*

7. Things are actually a bit more complicated than this. In some cases, being transparent, or openly communicating with someone, is (partly) *constitutive* of respecting them. In those cases, we might regard being transparent as of non-instrumental value, or at least as more than merely instrumental value.

Chapter 6

1. Aristotle, "Now in everything the pleasant or pleasure is most to be guarded against; for we do not judge it impartially," in *Nicomachean Ethics*, W. D. Ross, trans., revised by J. L. Ackrill and J. O. Urmson (New York: Oxford University Press, 1984), Book II.9.

2. Uri Berliner, "Wells Fargo Admits to Nearly Twice as Many Possible Fake Accounts—3.5 Million," NPR, August 31, 2017, https://www.npr.org/sections/thetwo-way/2017/08/31/547550804/wells-fargo-admits-to-nearly-twice-as-many-possible-fake-accounts-3-5-million.

INDEX

ACKNOWLEDGMENTS

This book lives at the end—or hopefully, the middle—of a journey I didn't see coming and didn't know I was preparing to make. I've taken too many steps to recount them all here, and I've been enabled to take the trip by more people than I can remember. But some stand out.

Brad Cokelet and Guha Krishnamurthi took the time to read the entirety of this manuscript and provided invaluable feedback. I hereby acknowledge that, to the extent these pages contain any misleading or just plain false statements, they are the appropriate objects of blame.

Alex Grzankowski and Eric Vogelstein. I asked both to read the manuscript and they refused. One must acknowledge their abject failure at friendship. Two other people made the commitment but didn't read it, though I have to acknowledge that I'm not nearly close enough with them to facetiously call them out by name. My only regret in life is that they probably won't read this either, and so neither guilt nor shame shall visit them.

Blair Beyda, Brent Weisenberg, Eric Corriel, Eric Siwy, David Palmer, and Jared Dietch are all wonderful people and have had an enormous positive impact on my life. One must acknowledge, however, their relatively minimal impact on this book.

My grandparents Rita and Herb Diamond (aka "Gee-Gee" and "Poppy") were simultaneously possessed of a great intensity and lightness of heart. They'd stare you down and call bullshit, and in the next breath, they'd crack a joke. They were curious. They pushed the envelope. They looked at things differently. They were irreverent. My editor, the wonderful Scott Berinato, spoke frequently about my "voice" in this book. But it's not my voice. It's Gee-Gee and Poppy's. They, and they alone, are to credit for my desire to dig deep into an issue and to blame for my lack of professionalism.

My parents—Randi and Brad Blackman—instilled in me an entirely unreasonable degree of confidence that forbids me from thinking I can't do something, like getting a PhD in philosophy, landing a job afterward in a terrible market, and starting and growing, of all things, an ethics consultancy. Their continual belief in me and their borderline maniacal love has been, and will always be, the ground I stand on.

On our first international trip together, when we were still dating, my wife and I rented a car in a relatively obscure city in Peru. After colliding with a motorcycle carrying two people and being placed in a police car, the officer asked if I had been drinking. Leah (aka "Tootz"), who was in the back seat, immediately became infuriated. "No, nunca!" she exclaimed. Eight years later, when I decided to leave academia and start a business, she earned the income without which I wouldn't have had the ramp I needed to build it. And if she didn't take care of our two young children on the weekends that I worked on this book, you wouldn't be reading these words right now. In all things, if I can move forward, it's only because she has my back.

ABOUT THE AUTHOR

REID BLACKMAN, PhD, is the CEO and founder of Virtue, where he works with companies to integrate ethical risk mitigation into the development and deployment of artificial intelligence and other emerging technologies. Reid was a founding member of Ernst & Young's Artificial Intelligence Advisory Board, and he volunteers time to the nonprofit Government Blockchain Association, where he is the Chief Ethics Officer.

Prior to founding Virtue, Reid was a professor of philosophy at Colgate University and the University of North Carolina, Chapel Hill. He also founded a fireworks wholesaling company and was a flying trapeze instructor. He received his BA from Cornell University, his MA from Northwestern University, and his PhD from the University of Texas, Austin.

He has contributed to *Harvard Business Review* and *TechCrunch*, his work was profiled in the *Wall Street Journal*, and he speaks at events and businesses around the world.